LENS

X

FRONT LINE. OURS

The Unreturning Army

www.**transworldbooks**.co.uk

The Unreturning Army

A Field Gunner in Flanders 1917–18

HUNTLY GORDON

with a foreword by
SIR MORTIMER WHEELER

Doubleday

LONDON · TORONTO · SYDNEY · AUCKLAND · JOHANNESBURG

TRANSWORLD PUBLISHERS
61–63 Uxbridge Road, London W5 5SA
A Random House Group Company
www.transworldbooks.co.uk

First published in Great Britain
in 1967 by J. M. Dent & Sons Ltd
Revised and extended edition published in 2013 by Doubleday
an imprint of Transworld Publishers

A CIP catalogue record for this book
is available from the British Library.

ISBN 9780857521675

Addresses for Random House Group Ltd companies outside the UK
can be found at: www.randomhouse.co.uk
The Random House Group Ltd Reg. No. 954009

The Random House Group Limited supports the Forest Stewardship Council®
(FSC®), the leading international forest-certification organisation. Our books
carrying the FSC label are printed on FSC®-certified paper. FSC is the only
forest-certification scheme supported by the leading environmental
organisations, including Greenpeace. Our paper procurement policy
can be found at www.randomhouse.co.uk/environment

Typeset in 11/14pt Sabon by
Falcon Oast Graphic Art Ltd.
Printed and bound in Great Britain by
Clays Ltd, Bungay, Suffolk

2 4 6 8 10 9 7 5 3 1

To the Memory of the Centre Section Gunners
of A Battery, 112th Brigade,
Royal Field Artillery,
Meteren

. . . Sad, smoking, flat horizons, reeking woods,
And foundered trench-lines volleying doom for doom.

O my brave brown companions, when your souls
Flock silently away, and the eyeless dead
Shame the wild beast of battle on the ridge,
Death will stand grieving in that field of war
Since your unvanquished hardihood is spent.
And through some mooned Valhalla there will pass
Battalions and battalions, scarred from hell;
The unreturning army that was youth;
The legions who have suffered and are dust.

From 'Prelude: The Troops' by Siegfried Sassoon

Contents

PREFACE

A shorter version of this book about the First World War was first published in 1967. My father wrote that he offered it for 'those who wanted to know, without reading volumes of history, what it was really like to be there on the spot'.

It certainly won approval from those who had been there. An ex-gunner wrote that it was 'by far the most vivid, accurate and moving account of the life we led'. An infantryman confirmed the peculiarly tough lot of the field gunner: 'after six months at Ypres we had nearly grown web feet: but if we were sorry for ourselves, we were even sorrier for the 18-pounder batteries in the forward area'. And his old friend the war artist Keith Henderson wrote, 'Dear Huntly – well done! But those nightmares, you have revived them, and what I have tried these many years to forget is as vivid and lurid as ever . . .'

And yet this is no misery memoir. If it makes you weep, like the best Shakespearian tragedy it also makes you laugh out loud. It is, *inter alia*, a testimony to the human spirit; it should perhaps be required reading for those dead-eyed politicians who believe that the accumulation of wealth is the sole motivator of humanity. That doesn't feature here at all, unless you count pinching cigars from the Bapaume canteen . . .

As the twentieth century drew to a close, the medal ribbons of the Great War faded from Remembrance Day services. But although the last veterans had marched away, interest in this extraordinary period lived on. Heartened, I took a deep breath and delved into my father's archive.

I found that the original book had been half as long again. The editing had distilled it well, but some passages on the 'cutting-room floor' cried out to be reinstated in the new edition. Some are simple explanations of how things worked; some are touching vignettes about the minutiae of life, and of working with horses; and two or three longer insertions fill gaps in the winter of 1917/18 – and, above all, include his shattering account of the massive German Spring Offensive in 1918, when we came close to losing the war.

I found fragments of another tale waiting to be heard, too: the story of the aftermath, and how these experiences affected a young man in the decade after the war – now added in a postscript.

Although the letters in this book were written without thought of publication, my father must have known that he was seeing history in the making. (Even his formidable mother's keen interest cannot wholly justify the breadth of detail!) He said later, 'they do not abound in "blood and guts" descriptions, for we who had lived through those experiences felt a certain restraint in writing about them . . . But a good deal can also be read between the lines. Matters of purely family interest have been omitted; here and there gaps have been filled to make a more consecutive narrative.'

How, fifty years on, did he recall the 'gaps'? At the bottom of his old chest I found the final treasure: a 'Brampton's Patent Instantaneous Binder', containing a modestly typed narrative entitled 'From Ypres to Somme'. At the end was the date – November 1918. He had written it before the echo of the guns had died away, when most of these events were less than a year old; and I realised that it forms the basis of the text around his letters in the present book. It wholly justifies his comment that these words come 'fresh from the battlefield itself – a last "live broadcast" before the memory of those devastating years fades into the pages of the history books'.

It is indeed history now: but the freshness remains.

David Gordon
Allowenshay, Somerset
August 2013

Foreword to the 1967 Edition

We stood, Huntly Gordon and I, upon a densely wooded hilltop in Normandy with an aged artillery 'director' (War Office disposals, £3) between us. It was August 1938, and we had known each other for several years. In vacations we would forgather, and with this familiar instrument of World War I, he would survey for me whatever archaeological site was my peaceful battlefield for the moment. The more entangled and impossible the scene, the more sturdily and resourcefully would Huntly tackle his task. On this occasion he allowed himself to murmur that 'anyway it wasn't as bad as Passchendaele'. Then he characteristically got on with the job.

Passchendaele. It figures largely in these pages but we scarcely mentioned the sombre name. We had both been gunners and we knew vaguely that we had both been in the battle; but war-talk was not our habit and we did not concern ourselves with chronicle. Passchendaele is not a name to bandy lightly, and half a century after its tragic folly the thought of it still beggars tolerance.

But now I have in front of me this transcription of Huntly's wartime letters to his mother, and with them a request for a foreword. I accede for two reasons: my friendship for Huntly, and my warm respect for an unaffected but affecting account of a peculiarly tense and in its way peculiarly human episode. Here is no theatrical over-statement, no writing pretty; here is a plain imprint of the daily horror which thousands of young men, fresh from school or workshop, endured with astonishing selflessness in that terrible autumn of 1917, amidst all those square miles of suppurating slime. Those who know only World War II have no inkling of the squalor and criminal incompetence which combined to return so much amiable humanity to its native clay. It is salutary that this convinc-ing and undemonstratively poignant record of Huntly's should be perpetuated.

At the time of Passchendaele, Huntly and I did not yet know each other, but we were actually very near neighbours in that grisly salient and, as a youthful battery commander, my case was closely similar to his. For his Bellevaardebeek I had my Steenbeek, beside (and largely under) which lay my ill-conditioned gun-pits, full to the brim with all manner of contamination. The layers sat in water, the guns recoiled into water. The gunners, thinned by wholesale casualties to cadre strength or less, were voiceless and red-eyed through cold and gas and sleeplessness. Now and then, we laughed defensively but with no sort of conviction. Now and then, men quietly wept ... I need not anticipate; the ridge of Passchendaele was the definition of hell.

But for Huntly and myself Passchendaele did one thing: it showed us both the nadir of misery above which all other physical tribulation has subsequently risen and must rise. The omniscient Byron knew:

> Through many a clime 'tis mine to go,
>   With many a retrospection curst;
> And all my solace is to know,
>   Whate'er betides, I've known the worst.

I will add only that in one small respect Huntly had it better than I. From my reading of the pages that follow, I see that he had very sensibly armed himself with *Pickwick Papers* when he went into action. By coincidence, so had I. But alas, my own little leather-bound volume was behind me in the ration-wagon when I stepped off it into the mud to take over my battery. A minute later there was a splitting crash and the wagon was replaced by a large new shell-hole . . . Since then I have never quite had the heart to re-read *Pickwick*. In one way and another, Passchendaele drew an abrupt dividing line across my experience (as across that of so many others), and I cannot pay higher testimony to the present book than to say that for an hour or two it has broken through that barrier and in a sense reintegrated past and present. It is a convincing personal document, and in so being it is a genuine fragment of the history of our time.

Sir Mortimer Wheeler
Burlington House, January 1967

CHAPTER ONE

A Sprig of Heather

I never meant to be a soldier. Like Ferdinand the Bull I would far sooner have been left to sit dreamily under a shady tree enjoying the perfume of the wild flowers. No blood and sand for me!

I was born into a Perthshire manse in 1898, a small end product of good Queen Victoria's golden reign, when all the world was fair. But in spite of my early inclination for a quiet life, the Fates seem to have had other ideas – even from the beginning.

Thus my first clear recollection is of stamping round the day-nursery, firing a pop-gun and shouting 'Bang, Kruger!' It was at the time of the South African War, and Kruger was of course that shifty patriarch in black frock-coat and top-hat who was President of the Boer Republic. Shortly after this Kruger fled, leaving the war to be carried on for a further two years by other Boer leaders who appear to have escaped my notice.

Not long afterwards I found myself fighting at the battle of Spion Kop. My brother, four years older, of course impersonated the dauntless British defending the mound of that name in the Manse garden. To me was allotted the unpopular role of the attacking Boers. I duly advanced up the slope and on hearing him shout 'Bang! You're dead,' fell in a death agony on the lawn. Unfortunately my neck cast a shadow over the entrance to an underground wasps' nest, so that the enraged occupants emerged in a swarm and made my agony a very lively one. Grown-ups carried me yelling to the laundry and daubed me with the blue-bag; and I lived to fight another day.

My interest in gunnery began at the age of three, when a party of wounded soldiers, invited to tea at the Manse, brought with them a gun-carriage on which was mounted a new Vickers-Maxim gun. This was much admired, as being the latest weapon. My task was to stagger round with a large tin of biscuits, which was almost too big for my short arms to grip. As a reward they lifted me up on to the gun, and promised that I too could be a gunner when I grew up.

My father, when a young man, had served as private secretary to his father when he was Lord Advocate and Secretary of State for Scotland. This early experience of legal and political affairs fitted my father to play a useful part in the union of the various Scottish Churches which was taking shape at the turn of the century. He was therefore persuaded to leave his Perthshire parish and work at the Church of Scotland headquarters in Edinburgh. To combine life in the country with his work in Edinburgh, my mother built a house on the golf links at North Berwick. This chain of events had its effect even on me. It was decided that I should be sent to the nearest school. Thus it was that I found myself a pupil at the Dunardarigh School for Girls.

At this school they taught me to weave together strips

of coloured paper, and to paint stylised flowers having four yellow petals and a long green stalk. The girls giggled at my efforts, as well they might. But I was more interested in the wild flowers in the fields on my way to school. There was also a horse to feed through the gate, and little wild strawberries by the wayside. All this took time, anything from one to two hours in fact, though the distance was only half a mile. As neither my mother nor my mistress believed the reasons I gave for being late, a small black notebook was put in my satchel in which columns had been ruled:

Huntly left home at .... a.m.
Huntly reached school at .... a.m.

Thus I carried my badge of shame and servitude with me. Hesitating at forgery, I could see nothing but to accept this first increase in the tempo of existence, a process which has continued over the years until it has latterly reached the speed of the rat-race about which so many people now complain. They have the sympathy of one who is at last free once more to look along the hedgerows for wild strawberries.

Before long, in the search for more advanced schooling, we moved to Edinburgh; and, my father being now much occupied with the work of church union, it was my mother who directed our education. For some reason she chose again to send me to another girls' school, Lady Margaret's, where I attended classes in fan-dancing. This, I should perhaps explain, consisted of graceful rhythmic movement to music, with a fan. There may have been other subjects, but they did not interest me nearly so much. After a term of this my mother, feeling quite rightly that I was rather young to make the most of the opportunities offered by Lady Margaret's, sent me to join my brother at Merchiston Castle Preparatory School, and my real education then began.

Private tuition by a governess had already carried me well beyond the 'C-A-T spells cat' stage. Now my mother, crowding on the pressure, engaged a spinster lady with breastplate corsage and protruding eyes to teach me the piano. She was terribly frustrated at my slow-motion rendering of the 'Merry Peasant', and kept hitting me over the knuckles with a pencil. I retaliated by coming home late from school, so that the music lessons became gradually shorter and more futile; and it was at last accepted that I was no infant Handel.

Life at school was much more interesting. Two other boys accepted me into a Secret Society. We met in a lean-to shack where in a dim light we melted lead and poured it over a carved piece of wood to form three plaques bearing the letter S, a talisman which we furtively showed to each other in class. A golden sovereign given me by my Uncle John went on the purchase of an air-gun with which we took it in turn to shoot sparrows. These we impaled on pen-nibs and roasted over a gas-jet. They smelt good, but were never cooked through; and our one attempt to eat them was enough.

When I was thirteen it was decided that the toughness of my Scottish education should now be refined by the softer cultural influence of an English public school. At least that was the idea. My mother selected Clifton, because the son of a Scottish minister whom we knew was head of one of the houses and would help me to feel at home there. But things did not work out that way. The head of the house knew, and I knew, that if it became known that he was looking after me, I would never live it down. So during my first term, which was also his last, we avoided each other like the plague, and I had to find my own feet in a strange new world.

That Clifton was a very different place from Merchiston I discovered on my first morning in chapel. During the prayers, I leaned forward, as is the Scottish custom, but did not actually kneel down like the rest. This had the additional advantage of keeping my new black trousers off the dirty floor. Suddenly I received a vicious poke on my behind with the point of an umbrella, and on turning round saw a furious bearded face glaring at me from above a parson's dog-collar. 'Kneel down,' he hissed. 'Don't you poke me,' I retorted with indignation, pushing his umbrella away. And there the matter stayed; until at the end of the morning my form-master, a Scot with a sense of humour, called me to him and asked for my version of the stinging report that had reached him. I asked rather hotly if it was right that I should be forced to abandon the customs of the church of my fathers at the point of an umbrella. To which he replied, 'Laddie, you're in Rome now. In things that don't matter, it's as well to do as the Romans do.' Thereafter I conformed to the extent of resting one knee lightly against a clean hassock. The Church Militant relaxed. The umbrella remained in its sheath.

My mother had not yet given up her dream of bringing out her musical talent in me. My debut as a pianist having ignominiously failed, a violin was bought for fifteen pounds. Four half-hour practices and one hour's lesson were required of me each week. After five years of this, my playing remained an ordeal alike for the listener and for myself; my theme song, appropriately, the 'Chanson Triste'. When I left school the violin was sold for fifteen pounds, a surprisingly good price considering all it had undergone at my hands. But those hours were not wholly wasted. They helped me to appreciate music; so long as it was played by others.

By contrast, my time in the choir was altogether well spent. Singing lifts the heart, and the choir practices often brought me comfort when I was oppressed by the loneliness of those early days. Even our monotonous daily confession, intoned by the choir at morning prayers, that we had erred and strayed like lost sheep (as if we cared!) had a soothing effect, until in time it became pleasantly meaningless.

The Clifton psalm-book contained many lovely chants by composers ranging from Thomas Tallis to Sir Herbert Oakeley. Our favourite psalm was the 104th, so full of colour and excitement, a rich tapestry of vivid phrases such as only the men of King James' day knew how to weave. Its special popularity with us owed something to the Clifton Zoo across the road. When, at choir practice, we sang of 'the lions roaring after their prey', the very sound of their roaring floated in through the open windows. And as we wandered among the gorgeous flower-beds in the zoo we could actually watch 'the wild asses quench their thirst', and see for ourselves that, allowing for a little poetic licence, 'the high hills are a refuge for the wild goats, and so are the stony rocks for the conies'.

My third term – the summer of 1912 – was a memorable one, for it marked the fiftieth anniversary of the founding of the college. The occasion was one of brilliant sunshine, marquees, flags and free strawberries and cream. Even the parents were to be admired, as they fluttered their parasols and puffed their cigars. In the choir I sat next to the boy who sang the treble solo in the Commemoration Anthem, 'Let us now praise famous men'. He seemed surprisingly calm. When the great moment came, he sent his flute-like notes soaring up into the chapel roof, while I sweated with anxiety on his behalf.

A grand parade of the Cadet Corps was also held, augmented by contingents from other schools. We marched past that great hero of the Boer War, Field Marshal Lord Roberts, VC. Afterwards he made a speech, warning us of the need to be ready for a great war which he could see coming. But no one took him seriously. Like those other exhortations from the chapel pulpit to prepare ourselves for 'the battle of life', they seemed empty words, and anyway there was nothing we could do about it.

That summer saw the end of the sorrowful process by which I was weaned from my Edinburgh home. I no longer crossed off in my diary the number of days before I could go home again. My centre of gravity at last swung to the south. Home gradually became the place where one went for the holidays, and Clifton the place where life beckoned, offering a profusion of new interests.

And what a lovely place it was. The warm beauty of the buildings encircling the quadrangle; the long parapet on which one leaned to watch cricket on the pitch where W. G. Grace had often flashed his bat; the rich fragrance of the may trees on the Downs; the sea-breezes from the Bristol Channel, sweeping up the Avon Gorge; the suspension bridge from which one looked down giddily on the wheeling gulls, and the toy boats and trains moving far below; that same slow-flowing Avon which had borne the good ship *Hispaniola* outward bound for Treasure Island, with Long John Silver brooding mischief in her galley. The silver freshness of those early mornings when, with coat and trousers hurriedly pulled over our pyjamas, some of us raced to the open-air baths for a quick swim in the sunshine before the rest of the world was properly awake.

Late in 1912 and during 1913 I made a determined effort to keep a diary. On the date 12/12/12 I started by recording my age as 14¾, my height 5 feet 3¾ inches, weight 9 stone 10 lb, size 14½ in collars, size 6 in boots, and my telephone number as Edinburgh 1892. Useful information provided by the publishers included the facts that income tax stood at 14d in the pound; letters required a ½d stamp; and in London, four-wheeler cab fares were 6d a mile, and the charge for an hour's drive in a hansom was 2/6d.

Here are some of the diarist's personal entries:

18th Jan.	First day of term. Sold two rotten pictures to innocent new boy for 1/-. Got 3d for a picture I found in the passage.
21st Jan.	Fitting new lampshade, fused study lights. Did prep with candles.
25th Jan.	Crowd around fire made me late with Bevan's toast. To make up time, set it on fire, and scraped off carbon. Didn't look too bad, but he made me eat it and start again. Fussy devil.
2nd Feb.	Rev. A.B.C. preached on 'Can these dry bones live?' Apparently *his* can, but only just.
10th Feb.	News arrived of ill-fated Scott Expedition, which perished on 17th March last year. Scott, Wilson, Bowers, and Oates who walked out to his death to give the others a chance.
16th Feb.	Rev. Champagne, Vicar of St Mary's Redcliffe, preached a sparkling sermon. Not the usual sort of dry-rot one gets.
5th March	Burial service of Morris, who died suddenly from sucking a pen-nib. Corps lined route from Chapel to Gates. First, seven boys in uniform with rifles reversed. Then the coffin, carried shoulder high. Then the mourners. Lastly, School House. Very impressive.
19th March	Our boxers won 4 of the 6 weights in the Public Schools Boxing Competition at Aldershot. A record.
8th May	Rumour afloat that Rayner is going to make the Corps fairly sweat this term. Sent up to H.M. for a star for Latin prose. No star, too short.
20th May	Trestle-bridging with the Corps. Shoulder very sore from carrying logs. Absolutely I have not had five minutes to myself all day.
22nd June	Row with Barkworth and Peppin over a violin practice I dodged. Avoided a tanning by delicate bit of diplomacy.

23rd June	Tanned by Bevan for jumping on and breaking Leir's bed. Got four with a fives-bat. Told him it didn't hurt.
24th June	Fearful bruises, and can't sit down comfortably.
25th June	We got Rintoul's all out for 24. I got 5 wickets and 35 runs.
28th June	Beat School House. Most exciting. We equalised their score in last over of match. Our last man in hit a four, and was caught next ball.
4th July	Lined Whiteladies' road for King George's visit to Agricultural Exhibition on Downs. Stood for 3 hours in the morning, and 2 in the afternoon. King looked pretty bored as a Suffragette had just presented him with a petition. A very boring day for me also.

So closes this glimpse of a fifteen-year-old boy; and with it an epoch. For never again was our country to know a year promising the same happy assurance of settled peace. And before long many of us were to give everything we had in the attempt to win back that prize.

For the summer holidays of 1914, our family rented a house in Perthshire, at St Fillans on the shore of Loch Earn. No place could have been lovelier. Morning after morning brought hot sunny days, and as the mists lifted from the loch the dew-laden spiders' webs spangled the heather with diamonds. Yet, for me, there was something missing. I could not settle down to anything; and a vague uneasiness depressed me and would not easily be dispelled.

But one bright morning, as I walked along the loch-side road to fish in a sheltered bay, round the corner there came on a bicycle a girl of about fifteen in a short flimsy blue dress. And when I saw the tight-fitting bodice revealing her shapely young breasts I could not look away. Her blue eyes held mine for a moment as she passed by; but I was struck dumb, and could only watch in silence the receding figure, with the honey-coloured hair coiled in plaits behind her ears, and the slim waist that so invited me to slip an arm gently round it. Once she glanced back at me over her shoulder and nearly came off her bicycle; but presently she vanished round a bend in the road, and left me still gazing.

Much too disturbed to fish, I climbed up through the heather and, sitting down, tried to compose my thoughts. This was a new experience for me. At school, it is true, there had been the fumblings of youth after sexual adventure and harmless romance. In my first year I had even been kissed by an older boy, awkwardly and to our mutual embarrassment. And in the past year I in turn had gazed longingly at one or two girlish-looking boys in Chapel, and yet been much too shy ever to speak to them outside.

But now my imagination ran riot. What could I not do with that girl in my arms? Away modesty, away even morality! I would be a Casanova and a Lothario in one – if only I knew how they went about it. With a concentration quite new to me I planned every detail of our next meeting by the roadside; rehearsed my opening words in a dozen different forms, none of which seemed likely to commend me to her; imagined how she might reply, and what my next move should be. The difficulty would be to persuade her to lay aside her bicycle and come up with me into the heather; but I lost no time in selecting a sheltered carpet of golden moss in readiness for our love-making. But how to do all this without frightening her? Above all, how to conceal all this from my family? And would she ever guess that I would be by the loch-side at the same hour next morning? And what if it rained? I might never see her again! I was distracted at the thought and did not sleep much that night.

Next morning I was early at the loch-side and chose a place where the road skirted the stony shore and she would see me fishing (though she would hardly guess what I would be really fishing for). The day was fresh, with a nice ripple on the water; and to fill in the time and calm my thumping heart I started casting and playing the fly along the wavelets.

After a little while I glanced up and saw, almost hidden by the trees along the shore, a bicycle approaching. My hand continued casting, my brain whirled, and losing my footing I nearly fell into the loch; but I continued with my fishing. Presently the cycle wheels grated to a stop at the roadside. Before I could look round, a big trout swirled at the fly; and simultaneously the voice of Jimmy-the-Post announced, 'Ye're wanted at the Post Office. It's aboot the war!'

And that is how the Great War broke on me. I landed the trout, but I never saw my love again.

At St Fillans Post Office, Colonel Cameron, DSO, having emerged from retirement, and borrowed a table and chair, had sent word round the lochside by Jimmy-the-Post that he would be there to enrol volunteers and answer questions; and as no one had any idea of what lay in store for us, we were all glad to consult the colonel. He told us firstly to keep calm; that as far as he knew the Germans had not yet landed; and that in any case it would take some time for them to reach St Fillans. (No one doubted that this would be their first objective.) In ones and twos keepers and farm-labourers, coachmen and grooms arrived to volunteer their services and have their names taken. Eighteen was the age limit, so there was nothing for me.

But I began to read the papers. We heard that our army had landed in France; but there were no photographs in the press. Soon our troops met and defeated the Germans at Mons, and we began sticking little flags into maps to see what was happening. Mons was followed unaccountably by days of retreat; then further battles at Le Cateau, the Marne and the Aisne. The illustrated papers did their best to satisfy our curiosity with illustrations by artists who specialised in the technique of the Boer War.

My Uncle Fred was somewhere out there commanding the 19th Infantry Brigade. Everyone at St Fillans was knitting socks, rolling bandages and sending out parcels of comforts. I felt useless and out of place; and for the first time was really glad to get back to school for the autumn term.

Back at Clifton all was bustle and change. With Kitchener of Khartoum at the War Office and Winston Churchill at the Admiralty no one expected the war to last beyond Christmas. In the scramble to join up and not miss the fun, many of the senior term were absent from their places, having added something to their age to satisfy the recruiting sergeant.

> Now all the youth of England are on fire,
> And silken dalliance in the wardrobe lies . . .

How splendid some of them looked as they revisited the school to see how we were getting on without them. Harry Kirkwood, twice winner of the Public Schools Welterweight Trophy, turned up, scarcely recognisable as a private in the Irish Guards. His head was shaven and the peak of his cap was down on the bridge of his nose; the shine on his boots made us want to hide our own; and his heavy parade-ground tread contrasted oddly with the lightness of his step in the ring. Many of us thought it strange of him to join up in the ranks, instead of taking a commission. We were after all the Officers' Training Corps. But that was his choice, and he told me he was very happy in the ranks. Neither he nor the others could tell us much about the fighting, except that they were good at plunging bayonets into sacks of straw; and our curiosity to know what it would be like to be under fire had to be satisfied from the novels of G. A. Henty and Captain F. S. Brereton (*With Buller in Natal*, *With Roberts to Pretoria* and *One of the Fighting Scouts.*)

The Cadet Corps took precedence over games, a minor revolution in itself. A number of elderly masters did their bit by joining the Corps without hope of getting into the fighting. With grim satisfaction we watched them drilling with the rookies in the quad. It was a strange reversal of fortune for those of us who already bore stripes (on our arms!) to find before us the tyrant of the classroom, parading absent-mindedly in a dishevelled uniform that normally would call for instant punishment. But we were forebearing. To see men, so formidable in their rightful place, openly step down and assume the role of humblest recruit was so disarming that none of us had the heart to take advantage of it.

Much time was taken up in boot-cleaning, button-polishing, and scraping the mud of the Downs off our puttees. And those route marches! Twice a week, as well as on Sunday afternoons, singing marching songs of which the most popular described the anatomical oddities of John Brown's Baby, we plugged along the country roads at close on four miles an hour for as much as twelve miles at a time. Some of the younger ones fell out or had to have their rifles carried. The martinet who commanded the Corps was out to make us fighting fit, however prematurely. But he only tired us out, so that war began to lose some of its glamour. Presently, following complaints by parents, our Sunday afternoons once more became our own.

Rugger continued as before, for that also would make us fighting fit, and in a much less wearisome way. My early love for the game now bore fruit and, as a second-row forward with an aptitude for kicking goals, my name appeared in the top game, Whites v. Stripes; and finally took a regular place among the Whites. It was after the

Wellington match that H. S. Gammell,* the captain of the
1st XV, made my heart miss a couple of beats by taking me
quietly by the hand and saying, 'Congratulations on your
cap!' I was so overcome that I told no one about it. It was
the first time I had won success at anything. And when a
small box arrived for me from Steer and Geary, I wedged a
chair against my study door-handle, unwrapped the crinkly
tissue paper and gazed with rapture on this lovely cap of
deep blue velvet with its braid and tassle of silver. And when
I put it on and looked in the mirror to see the tassle swing,
it was a moment of awestruck ecstasy.

Lord Kitchener now called for a vast volunteer army to
enlist for 'three years or the duration of the war'. Our hopes
of victory in a month or two were snuffed out like a candle.
It was as if the runner of a race, having set off to do a fast
quarter-mile, were suddenly told the distance had been
changed to three miles. Half unbelieving, we had to adjust
ourselves to a different view of the future. My part in the
war would not come for another two years, and what I was
learning in the meanwhile would not be needed then. Much
study, the Preacher had said, was a weariness of the flesh. It
would also be pointless. So I took care not to work too
hard.

Then one morning we noticed a piece of paper, pinned
to the chapel door. It read: 'Killed in action: A. E. J. Collins,
Captain, Royal Engineers.' That name to us was a legend,
for its bearer had made the highest score in the history of
cricket, and on our Clifton ground. I had thought of him as
one of the Ancients in a furry top-hat, defending something
like a croquet hoop with a prehistoric type of bat. It came
as a shock to discover that he had only left the school twelve

---

* Scholar of Pembroke College, Cambridge. Captain, Gordon
Highlanders; mentioned in Dispatches; Military Cross. Killed in
Action 1918.

years ago, and was now lying dead in France. Later we became hardened to these reminders of mortality; but that first death-blow against one of the immortals was hard to accept.

By degrees the school settled down to a wartime routine. The food deteriorated; meat, butter and eggs were short. Some said this was due to the German submarine blockade of our island; others mischievously suggested it was due to the stinginess of the housemasters who fed us.

In April 1915, at a place called Ypres, the Germans loosed a fresh horror upon the world when they released clouds of poison gas against our men. Surprise was complete and many choked to death in the froth that welled up from their bursting lungs. The gas was identified as chlorine. For an on-the-spot antidote our soldiers were advised to piddle on their handkerchiefs (if any) and tie them over nose and mouth. No doubt they replied in suitable terms. Curiosity prompted me to produce some chlorine in the Chem. Lab. The book said this could be done by mixing hydrochloric acid with potassium permanganate. I did this, but nothing seemed to happen; so to hurry things up I warmed the test-tube over a Bunsen flame and took a deep sniff. When they had picked me off the floor, two boys helped me back to my study, where for some hours I crouched over the warm pipes shivering from the shock and barely able to draw breath. The wheezing passed off in a couple of days, but I treated chlorine with respect after that.

The summer term of 1915 came, and with it cricket. To me this game had hitherto been an excuse for a lazy afternoon with a book under the trees. I thought it would be much better played with a soft ball. But during the previous summer I had begun to bowl fast, for the fun of it, and thus began to find there was something to the game after all.

This year I made the chance discovery that if the ball were held in a certain way it would suddenly change its mind in mid-flight and swing off the wicket towards first slip. Why it did this was a mystery as much to me as to those batsmen who obligingly snicked it off the edge of the bat into slip's hands.

This knack was brought to the notice of the games-master and others; and they coached me, so that the game really had to be taken seriously. My hands became hardened with practice on the slip-machine, and having a good eye I was able to put the bat to the ball and make a few runs. We were not a good side that year, and as no better fast bowler was available, my name appeared in the school 1st XI for the two-day match against Rugby. On that occasion my contribution to the score was negligible, but Alec Leslie, our captain, gave me the new ball and my headlong attack cost Rugby two of their best batsmen in each innings. All four were kind enough to snick me into the slips, and if looks could have killed I would have died four violent deaths in quick succession.

But my satisfaction was short-lived. Late on the first day, the easiest of catches spooned up to me at mid-off dropped like a poached egg between my feet. The batsman went on to make a century. O deepest shame! It would have been a relief to be led off the field in handcuffs. That is the trouble with cricket. It is an emotionally violent game, but you cannot give vent to your feelings; which is perhaps why the Scots are no good at it. To my surprise, I was given my colours for this match.

With 'Business as Usual' for the national slogan, we thus settled down to our lessons and games, leaving the future to take care of itself. Our life at school was comfortably insulated from reality. The Kaiser with his upturned moustaches and musical comedy uniform was a cartoonists' figure of fun, though often, too, a bloodstained ogre devouring women and children. We hated the helmeted jack-booted image of Germany, and the use of poison gas was a real cad's trick – but what could you expect from such an arrogant people?

Latterly, however, the war had taken on a grimness that could not be ignored. Battle after battle brought no result – Mons, the Marne, Ypres; and then, in the effort to break the siege of trench warfare, Neuve Chapelle, Festubert and Loos, with lengthening casualty lists and no results to show for them.

Geoffrey Robinson, who was old enough to get a commission in the 10th Gloucesters at the outbreak of war, wrote to me full of enthusiasm during his first spell in the trenches at Loos. His letter was still in my pocket when I saw his name on the chapel door. His mother sent me a letter from a corporal in his regiment. It said, 'I can assure you he died, as he always lived, a real gentleman. All the men would do anything for him. He was leading his men and cheering them on.' Poor gentle, uncomplicated, gallant Robbie!

A fortnight later his mother sent me his silver pencil as a keepsake. From her letter I learned that her other son, not at Clifton, was also killed in the same attack. She was a frail little person, and her heart must have died that day; but her letter gave no sign of it.

In such ways it began to come home to us that this was quite a new kind of war; not just for the eager few, but for us all. With the German submarine blockade tightening its grip, in spite of all that the Fleet could do, the future was dark and the end uncertain. The only certainty was that we must keep on keeping on, because anything else was unthinkable. The first gallant impulse that had moved men in their hundreds of thousands to stand in queues at the recruiting offices had almost spent itself. Not that the ideals which brought them there had changed; they were indeed unchangeable. But the spare manpower was exhausted, and for the first time compulsory service was openly discussed.

In a last effort to raise more volunteers, the Clifton Cadet Corps went on a route march through Bristol with our band playing. The procession was augmented by detachments from St John Ambulance, the Fire Brigade and any other uniformed bodies who were willing to march with us. We finished up at College Green under the benign gaze of Queen Victoria's statue. There, as a platoon commander, I had a front-rank view of the proceedings. The Lord Mayor in his robes addressed the assembled crowd. His speech was followed by another rousing call from a white-haired general with rows of medals and a plumed hat. The sergeant in the recruiting marquee sharpened his pencil expectantly; and we waited for the rush. After a long silence, one seedy little man with rounded shoulders shambled forward.

My last year at school was a time of growing discord between what would have been the rich harmony of school life and the brassy clash of the war. They made me an officer in the Cadet Corps, a promotion that I did not greatly value. On the other hand, I must admit to feeling elated, if a little surprised, at finding myself Vice-Captain of the Rugger XV, Captain of the Cricket XI, and winning a cup and a cauliflower ear as a boxer. But self-conceit has always seemed to me a most objectionable quality; and in any case the thought of what others were enduring in France made school achievements look rather small.

It was good to be a Praepostor in the sixth form, to enjoy the personal friendship of some of the masters, and to eat muffins and read poetry beside their study fires. It pleased me, too, that mine could be the hand that gave the coveted cricket colours to others who had earned them. We, the exalted ones, and only we, had the distinction of walking with hands in pockets and blazer collars turned up; nor would any others have dared to usurp that bizarre privilege.

Thus most of us played hard and worked a trifle absent-mindedly, with one eye on the war. No more was there an eagerness not to miss it. By now we knew too much, and were ready to offer ourselves at the proper time, not before. The lists on the chapel door were getting longer, and gave the names of boys who had been our seniors barely a year before. Among them was that of my first study companion, Nevill Young.*

Our house-group photograph of 1912 shows forty boys. By the end of the war thirteen were dead, fifteen had been wounded, some more than once, and only twelve had come through physically unharmed. In later years I have often walked through the Memorial Archway, and with breaking heart read names that, in their alphabetical order, seem to re-echo the roll-call of my time. I wonder what Field-Marshal Earl Haig (OC) thought when he unveiled it after the war. But in the summer of 1916, the death-mill was not yet running at full speed. The Somme, and Passchendaele and many other blood-soaked names were not yet known to us. We were as yet only nearing that period of the war of which it was written, 'Death was on the door-step in those days, seizing very greedily those who went out, and waiting for those who were to come.'

* 2nd Lieutenant, Royal Sussex Regiment. Killed in Action 1916.

CHAPTER TWO

Kitchener Wants YOU!

It was the afternoon of Wednesday, 7th June 1916. In the still air the lime trees along College Road hung heavy with fragrance and murmurous with bees. On the far side of the cricket ground the warm red sandstone of the school buildings and the huge copper lantern crowning the chapel formed a background rich in colour and design. Stretched on their rugs under the limes, several hundred Clifton boys were casually watching the cricket; some busy with books, some with bags of cherries, some intent on the play; others, with straw hats tilted over their noses, lay dreaming the dreams of youth. The day was something of an occasion, for Lord Hawke, England's test captain of the nineties, had brought down an MCC team to play our 1st XI, and the whole school had turned out to watch these cricketing giants of the past. Palairet of Somerset, Hornby of Lancashire, A. J. L. Hill, the Hampshire captain, Miller, the Wiltshire captain – six England caps and two county professionals – they were names to fire the imagination and attract many passers-by who stopped to look over the palings of College Road. And now Lionel Palairet, that most graceful of batsmen, had played himself in, and the runs were coming freely.

I was fielding at point, and, like the rest of the school eleven, was on my toes. It really was fascinating to watch the poised stance, easy and relaxed, the unhurried lift of the bat, the apparently effortless swing that, with steely wrists and perfect timing, sent the ball cracking past cover point to the boundary. I had just edged away a yard or two, so that I might have time to get protective hands to any square cut directed at my midriff, when the unusual sound of a news-boy's cry was heard down College Road. At first I thought I had mis-heard him; but the cry was repeated, 'Lord Kitchener drowned! Lord Kitchener drowned! Special!'

Play stopped. It seemed unbelievable, perhaps some stupid joke. The great father figure of the war must surely be, as he always had been, at the War Office. How could he be drowned? Then those few who had secured a paper passed on the appalling news. It was heard with deep mis-givings, presumably by all, certainly by me. The match was resumed; and ended, I forget how. Rather perfunctorily we all cheered the famous men as they left. Then there was time for thought.

Inglorious though the admission may be, I had been hoping that somehow the Allies might win the war before the end of my last term, and I might go on to Oxford. But with this disastrous loss of the great Lord Kitchener, who towered above all others as our war leader, that hope finally expired. There would be no early end to the war now.*

* Lord Kitchener was aboard the armed cruiser HMS *Hampshire* when it sank after striking a mine during a storm off the Orkneys on 5 June 1916.

The facts had therefore to be faced; and I realised without much enthusiasm that at the end of the term I and my contemporaries would have to choose what to do. From old posters on the hoardings the late Lord K. still fixed me with his hypnotic stare – *vultus instantis tyranni** – still pointed his gloved finger at me and, from under a moustache even more magnificent than the Kaiser's, announced, 'Your Country Needs YOU!' Well, of course.

But on two things I was determined. Firstly, being no sailor, I would fight on land. Secondly, those dreary route marches with our Cadet Corps having given me a distaste for long walks, I must find some way of going to war on a horse. And I might as well do the thing in style, professionally. The obvious course was to try for a regular commission in the Royal Field Artillery.

Fortunately there was still just time to enter my name for the Royal Military Academy, Woolwich, and sit the examination at the end of the term; and this I did. The standard no doubt had been lowered and it was a pleasant surprise to learn that the examiners would accept my level of Greek as an alternative to Higher Mathematics, which latter subject was utterly beyond me. Both subjects seemed equally irrelevant to the killing of Germans with field-guns. At any rate my name duly appeared on the pass list and I was instructed to report at Woolwich in September.

At the end-of-term service in the chapel, when, according to custom, the whole school joined in glorious unison to sing that fine old German hymn, 'Now Thank We All Our God', I could not sing a note. Clifton had come to mean so much. It was with a heavy heart that I said goodbye to my friends, and turned away from the place of boyhood's dreams and their fulfilment.

*

* 'The threatening countenance of the tyrant'! (Horace)

At the end of summer term, I went to camp at Tidworth with the Clifton OTC, the Officers Training Corps. As a platoon commander, no longer having to carry a rifle, I was looking forward to less drudgery and more fun at this my last camp.

The programme exceeded our expectations. Contingents from many famous public schools were there, and we were given demonstrations of every aspect of warfare. We put on gas masks, hesitatingly entered a tent full of chlorine gas, and were relieved to find ourselves unaffected by it. We fired Stokes mortars, watching the projectiles shoot up into the air and land with a satisfying crash in a nearby quarry. We worked field telephones, sat in the cockpit of an old aeroplane, and generally had an exciting and useful ten days of it.

But the biggest thrill was reserved for the last day when we found ourselves being briefed for night operations. On Tidworth Plain the Sappers had constructed an exact reproduction of a section of the opposing German and British trench systems – front line, support, and communication trenches complete in every realistic detail.

We were warned that at the right moment canisters of ammonal would explode overhead without hurting us. Some of us were supplied with harmless hand grenades, known as 'potato bombs'. These turned out to be a baked-clay imitation of a Mills bomb containing a small charge of gunpowder, with a short stick of protruding fuse. One had to strike a match, get the fuse burning and count three before throwing it. It would explode one second later with an exciting but relatively harmless puff of smoke and flame. Failure to count three would give an enterprising enemy a chance to field it, and make a hot return to the wicket!

It was all very realistic and a great credit to the producers. Under cover of darkness I led my platoon up a communication trench and presumably reached the front line. At the appointed time, our bombing squad went quietly over the top and, meeting an enemy patrol in a huge mine crater, started to do business with them. Sparks were flying, and we heard cracks and puffs mingled with oaths and laughter. Then came the time for the main attack. We lined the parapet; and I waited tensely while the hand of my synchronised wristwatch crept round to zero hour.

On the dot of time whistles blew, up the ladders we went, and out into no-man's-land, while the barrage crashed deafeningly overhead. Several hundred cadets from rival schools charged excitedly forward, and a free fight for the honour of our respective schools was just beginning when the bugles blew the 'standfast', searchlights were switched on, and we all adjourned for hot cocoa. That night's operation was the most realistic piece of training that ever came my way. We thought it a pity that the war itself could not have been conducted on similar lines.

In September 1916 the war had entered a gloomier phase. The fighting on the Somme was producing casualty lists of unprecedented length, and the official communiqués revealed that positions were repeatedly changing hands, with very little progress at the end of it.

For obvious reasons the shortage of officers became suddenly acute. To meet the situation the normal training period of two years at Woolwich was compressed into a mere six months; though by the time I got there second thoughts had prevailed and the course was extended to nine months.

Meanwhile clothes had to be thought of.

The gentleman-cadets of the Royal Military Academy were required to arrive clad in lounge suits and bowler hats. Possessing neither of these things, I went to an inexpensive tailor in Edinburgh, chose a heavy grey tweed, was measured, and asked for the suit to be sent on by the date required. Unfortunately when I came to try it on just before leaving for London, the trousers turned out to be too long and too tight, and the coat too big. However, knowing that within a few weeks this sorry misfit would be replaced by a well-fitted uniform, I put a good face on it and presented myself at 'the Shop'.* The gates clanged, and I passed under military discipline.

The Royal Military Academy was at that time housed in a venerable building of Tudor style, overlooking Woolwich Common. Generations of officers of the Royal Engineers and the Royal Artillery had lived in it, trained in it, and passed out of it. For a building so steeped in history and military tradition – which may have accounted for the all-pervading aroma of carbolic and mice – modern sanitation may well have been considered out of place. At any rate, in the room which I shared with two Royal Engineer cadets, the only washing facilities consisted of a bucket of cold water and an enamel basin on a tripod stand. Thatcher, our joint servant, had a kettle and gas ring from which he was just able to provide each of us with one enamel mug of hot water for our morning ablutions. These and other Spartan conditions were no doubt designed to accustom us to hardship. They so far succeeded that before long we would have felt reasonably comfortable in any of His Majesty's jails.

On the first morning I was taking a look round when I was hailed by two officers who seemed to want to speak to me. I strolled over to them, and the following one-sided conversation took place in a voice rising finally to a shout:

'Stand to attention!'

'Who the hell do you think you are?'

'How dare you wear your trousers turned up? Take a check parade.'

* As R.M.A. Woolwich was known.

'Now get off, at the double.'

'Double, damn you! And KNEES UP!'

I fled.

When I reached my room, Thatcher, our soldier-servant, was there, and he enlightened me. It seemed that no one below the rank of under-officer could wear turned-up trousers; so a penknife cut the stitching and soon another 1½ inches was added to my overlong trouser legs. A check parade meant parading at the ghastly hour of six o'clock in the morning, immaculately turned out. Any defect, however small, such as a spot of dust on the bowler hat, would mean more check parades. Finally it was the privilege of any senior-term cadet to shout 'Double, damn you!' at any newly joined cadet, the idea being to bring home to us that we were 'snookers', the lowest form of military life, and that in public everything must be done at the run. Any failure to conform to these requirements would spell trouble. 'But don't you worry, Sir, you'll be all right!' Thatcher concluded with unconvincing optimism.

All this was in startling contrast to the leisurely dignity of my last term at Clifton. But at least I had the sense to see that this latest humiliation was only part of the moulding process that we all had to undergo in a community where, from now on, nothing counted but the badge of Army rank. This fact was presently brought home to us by the sergeant-instructors on the parade ground and elsewhere. Provided they addressed us as Mister or Sir, and abstained from obscene language, they could and did say pretty well anything they liked; and much of it was rich and fruity.

My particular squad was drilled by Sgt. Wagstaffe of the Grenadiers. God rest his soul! A grey-haired man, as stiff as a ramrod, he always appeared to be leaning backwards, as if in recoil from the series of explosions that we came to recognise as his words of command. Wielding a silver-topped cane, and addressing us in a voice like rending calico, he fairly tore us to shreds, but an occasional twinkle in his eye at the 'stand-easy' made ample amends. The weather was hot, the parade ground dusty, and I cursed that thick, ill-fitting tweed suit as the sweat trickled down from under my bowler hat.

Most of us had already been trained in infantry drill at school, and before long our performance was little short of the standard of the Guards themselves. Of course no one told us we were even satisfactory. But the rumour did reach us that in the Sergeants' Mess Sgt Wagstaffe had been offering to back his squad against all others. And one day when the under-officer of our company came to watch us drilling, we saw that his enquiries were met with a nod and a wink from 'Old Waggers' that told us all we wanted to know.

And there were other ways in which Woolwich sought to press us into the mould of the Regular Army officer, teaching us to be tough and relentless, to give and exact unquestioning obedience to orders. There was the 'Snookers Concert', designed to humiliate those who stood on their dignity, to bring home to us that we were just raw material, and to teach us to keep our tempers. At an evening session in one of the courtyards, the snookers had to appear one by one on a platform to do an 'act' in front of the two hundred members of the senior term. It could be a song, it could be one or two stories, funny or filthy or both. All alike were acclaimed with ironical applause, conflicting orders and jets from a fire-hose. I missed this audition, having both knees and one arm in bandages from a fall on the obstacle course. It was a relief to be told by one of the under-officers, whom I had met at school when playing football against Cheltenham, that my absence would not be noticed.

If our square-bashing was exacting, no less rigorous was our training in 'Equitation', an art of which I knew literally nothing. In preparation for this I had managed once to hire an off-duty cab-horse at North Berwick, but the experience taught me little more than that the middle part of a horse is safer than either end. The training at the Woolwich Riding School confirmed this profound truth, and it also added much to it in a very short time.

It was usually before breakfast that our squad marched at a quick-step down Academy Road, and through the lofty doors on to the silent tan of the riding school. There Captain Booker awaited us, superbly mounted on his chestnut mare. One of the finest riders in the country, he had represented Britain in a number of international championships. As a groom said to me, 'You should see him take his horse over jumps ringed in flame!' In short, a kind of male Valkyrie.

As we entered the arena, Captain Booker would run his eye over us with a faintly sardonic smile. Then followed an unvarying ritual.

'Squad, halt!' from our section commander; and 'Good morning, Sir!'

Captain Booker, with an old-world courtesy that did not entirely conceal the menace in his voice, would reply, 'Good morning, gentlemen! Are we all feeling bright and breezy, eh?', reining back his eager mare so that she reared up beautifully. 'Keen as mustard and no hangovers, eh? Very well, then.' (Actually far from well, that sinking feeling on an empty stomach!) Then – 'To your hosses, gentlemen, PLEASE!' The last word was barked out as the executive word of command. Till then, wait for it, not a flicker of an eyelid! But many sidelong glances were directed at the assembled ring of twenty or more horses, for we quickly got to know which kicked and bucked, which were a rough ride, and those blessed few that would take you round like an armchair.

It seemed to me that our riding school somewhat resembled the Colosseum of Ancient Rome, with the difference that in those days the group of early Christians stood waiting for the lions to be released at them, whereas now, with a similar anxiety, we latter-day saints waited to be released at the lions. On the command 'Please', we would dash in all directions, each to the horse of his choice. And in this game of musical chairs, those who were outstripped or outwitted ran along the line well knowing that the only seats left unoccupied would be the most uncomfortable ones. With here and there a word of advice or commiseration, the grooms would leave the arena.

'Everyone ready? Mount your hosses!' A heave up, leg swung over, feet into the stirrups, and we sit rigid.

'Right turn, walk-march, terr-rot!' and we are off.

Then the fun begins.

'Drop your reins and cross your stirrups! Roll your knees in and sit down in the saddle. Come, Mr B., straighten yourself up. You'll never make a horse-gunner. You look to me like an old wife sitting on a night-commode!' And so it went on. Urged on by sarcasm and quips from our ring-master, bucked and often dislodged by the horses, we gradually found our seats, and before very long could even take our jumps bareback, with folded arms and a fair chance of a graceful finish.

My favourite exercise was known as 'vaulting on and off on the near side'. Spurred heels clicked high in the air as you rolled off the saddle; three running paces, an upward twist, and you were back in the saddle again. Given a good horse, one only needed tights and spangles to rival any circus equestrienne. But if you were landed with a sixteen-hand mount or a kicker, you were left to plod round the ring, leaping up against the saddle repeatedly and in vain, until at last Captain Booker would relent, with the order, 'All right. Turn in.'

In addition to riding and 'square-bashing' there were many other ways in which our bodies were trained, exhausted and toughened. At physical training we had spring-heeled instructors whose bounding energy took little account of our occasional weariness. 'On the toes, on the toes!' they would cry whenever our prancings became flat-footed. They even taught us fencing, leaving us in the full lunge position till our muscles ached with cramp and the foils drooped to the floor. It did occur to some of us that a knowledge of this seventeenth-century form of combat might not help us much on the Western Front – but we supposed there must be some reason for it that we did not appreciate at the time. Still we could not help feeling that a truncheon or dagger might be of more practical use on a dark night in no-man's-land.

Our drill with bayonets and swords was limited to ceremonial saluting. It was not until I was in the trenches that I learned the other ways in which bayonets could be used. But gun-drill with 18-pounders was the real thing. We learned the patter by heart, and were soon efficient in every position on the gun. The competition for speed between rival gun-crews was intense, and anyone who was slow heard about it from the rest of the crew.

At the end of the day, there was still much to read up, and we had little time or energy left for extending our social experience by 'living it up', whether in grimy Woolwich or the West End. I did not drink or dance, and the experiences of some others seemed to show that women were a full-time hobby that would have to wait for more leisurely days. When the day's work ended at ten o'clock or so, I was glad to drop on my bed in full uniform and doze for a couple of hours, before getting undressed and into a single bed for the rest of the night.

But let it not be thought that our lives were lacking in colour. Someone high up had evidently decreed that to off-set the austerity of the curriculum something should be done to raise our morale. The result was the peculiar social function known as 'Saturday night Snookers' Dance'. It was voluntary, but of course we had to go. We were told to parade in the gym in zephyrs, white slacks and gym-shoes. There was some speculation beforehand as to who our partners might be – the debutantes of Woolwich? Or ladies of the town?

With lustful anticipation we duly reported at the gym. We found awaiting us a brass band from the barracks; also lemonade, but no ladies. The band struck up, and it then became apparent that the only lady partners were to be found among the gentlemen-cadets themselves. Not many of us could dance, but anything for novelty! And I was one of those who coyly let it be known that I was available as a lady. Of course the only difference was that, to martial music, the gentlemen marched firmly forward while we girls, surrendering to their manly embrace, marched seductively backwards to the accompaniment of comments that would have made a sergeant-major blush. It is just possible that towards the end of the evening, a trace of gin may somehow have got into the lemonade. At any rate the proceedings became boisterous and a good time was had after all.

One dark winter's evening, as my class sat puzzling over gunnery problems in terms of trigonometry, a great flash was seen through the windows. A few seconds later a concussion wave hit us, bringing part of the ceiling down. The explosion was in Siemens' Works at Silvertown. Seventy girls who were filling shells vanished in a flash. Next day some of us went over to have a look. But all that remained was a vast crater and a fantastic tangle of steel girders encrusted in thick ice where the water from the hoses had frozen. It was our first experience of the power of high explosive. It brought some much-needed reality into our textbook problems.

The sudden telescoping of the course from two years to six or nine months, following on the heavy casualties at the battle of the Somme, presented many problems. What should be retained, what curtailed, and what omitted, were questions that would have been better decided by those with up-to-date experience of conditions on the Western Front than by those of higher rank whose battle experience had been chiefly gained in the South African War. As it was, our syllabus was a strange hotch-potch, in which matters of urgent practical importance were often crowded out by non-essentials.

It was obviously right that we should spend time studying the ballistic problems of gunnery. But why were we filling up notebooks with the details of Wellington's Peninsular Campaign, the Principles of Strategy and Tactics – and the Administration and Organisation of units as big as divisions and army corps, of foreign armies as well as our own? And why did we spend hours on the chemistry of explosives, learning the chemical formulae, manufacturing processes, and relative merits of gunpowder, cordite, lyddite, ammonal and TNT? From such a menu we were allowed no choice. In due course we would fire what we were given, and probably be blown up by some German explosive of which we had never heard.

Battery drill on Woolwich Common was really a farce, when, instead of having jingling six-horse teams to pull the guns and limbers, we had to drill in make-believe fashion with wheelbarrows. The arrangement was that one cadet pulling a wheelbarrow represented a six-horse team and limber; another cadet pushing a second barrow in the track of the first one represented the gun. Although this demonstrated in the most cumbersome fashion the relative movements of the units composing the battery, we felt that pushing wheelbarrows about on a muddy common was a form of training more suited to gardeners than to artillerymen. Anyone who has been thrilled by the Royal Artillery Musical Ride at Olympia will understand our feelings. Once only did we have mounted battery drill on Woolwich

Common with borrowed horses and guns. That was also the only occasion when I had a chance to ride a horse outside the riding school, before going into action in France.

At the end of our training we paid a four-day visit to Larkhill Artillery Range on Salisbury Plain to fire the guns that we had so far only handled at gun drill on the square. Unfortunately, at that period of the war there was such a shortage of shells that we were only allowed three live rounds per gun-crew. It was therefore something of an occasion when each of these precious rounds was fired.

The muzzle velocity of an 18-pounder was 1,615 feet per second, or 1,100 miles an hour, one and a half times the speed of sound. We were astonished to hear that it was possible actually to see the shell moving at this supersonic speed just after it had left the gun. So our three rounds were fired by a skeleton crew, while the rest of us, gazing along the line of fire, caught a fleeting glimpse of a black dot as it vanished in the direction of the target.

It would have been useful to know something about German mentality and methods, their weapons and the various types of projectile that would shortly be hurled at us. I personally wished that some way could be found of converting my mild dislike of Germans into something nearer active hatred, which I was simple enough to think was an essential preliminary for killing Germans. What I was looking for was the psychological equivalent of the Indian War Dance, or 'Scots Wha Hae' and all that; something to stir the blood. But this kind of inspiration was entirely lacking in our training. It may have been thought un-English. Or could it perhaps have been that a convincing reason for the individual Britisher to kill the individual German did not really exist, and that we were only marionettes, made to dance to a tune played by others?

But our greatest need of all was for some experience in handling men. Most of us were 'sons of gentlemen', straight from the cloistered or blinkered life of public schools, who did not speak the same language or share the same interests as the men we were soon to command. The military machine took us in as schoolboys at one end, and churned us out as officers at the other. But it did nothing whatever to help us bridge this gulf. To know yourself as being green and inexperienced, and soon to be given responsibility for the lives of fifty or sixty men, mostly older and far more experienced, was indeed a disturbing thought. Later I often felt how unworthy I was of their uncomplaining obedience and loyalty. That they accepted such inadequate leadership was a proof of their generosity and tolerance. They had no option, I suppose, any more than I had. So we both put a good face on it, and a workable relationship was hammered out in the stress of war.

At last the great day came when the cadets of my term passed out at a ceremonial parade under the august eye of General Sir William Robertson, Chief of the Imperial General Staff. I received the parchment that was His Majesty's commission, and exchanged farewells with many friends and acquaintances, few of whom I was ever to see again. To little Thatcher, my servant, I said a very sincere goodbye, for I owed him more than he probably knew. No one could have taken greater pride in seeing that 'his gentlemen' were always turned out smartly. Our Sam-Browne belts and boots had reflected a shine second to none, which he achieved with his secret mixture of beer and boot-polish – and unflagging elbow-grease; and he had always been ready with advice and an inexhaustible fund of unprintable army stories, to help us as 'snookers' to find our feet, and to build us up as we rose to higher rank.

When the fuss and farewells were over, I chose a quiet

moment to open and read the document that was my commission. This is what it said:

GEORGE by the Grace of God, of the United Kingdom of Great Britain and Ireland, and of the British Dominions beyond the Seas, King, Defender of the Faith, Emperor of India, etc.

To our Trusty and well beloved Huntly Strathearn Gordon, Greeting: We, reposing especial Trust and Confidence in your Loyalty, Courage, and good Conduct, do by these Presents Constitute and Appoint you to be an Officer in Our Land Forces from the Sixth day of June, 1917. You are therefore carefully and diligently to discharge your Duty as such in the Rank of Second Lieutenant or in such higher Rank as We may from time to time hereafter be pleased to promote or appoint you to, of which a notification will be made in the London Gazette, and you are at all times to exercise and well discipline in Arms both the inferior Officers and Men serving under you and use your best endeavours to keep them in good Order and Discipline. And We do hereby Command them to Obey you as their superior Officer, and you to observe and follow such Orders and Directions as from time to time you shall receive from Us, or any other superior Officer, according to the Rules and Discipline of War, in pursuance of the Trust hereby reposed in you.

Given at Our Court, at Saint James's, the First day of June 1917 in the Eighth Year of Our Reign.

By His Majesty's Command

This impressive document bore the Royal Seal and was countersigned with a reproduction of the King's signature.

My first reaction was to think that His Majesty might have hesitated to repose 'especial Trust and Confidence' in me, had he known how little of it I had in myself.

Next morning I left 'the Shop', rather self-conscious in the well-fitting uniform of a 2nd lieutenant of the Royal Field Artillery, with an engraved sword of my own, and a very pretty line in highly polished field-boots and clinking spurs. Who, at the age of nineteen, would not have worn them with pride, and a determination to prove right trusty, come what may?

Short though it was, ten days' embarkation leave was enough for a round of visits to friends and relations at home, and for some hurried purchases of equipment. The resplendent field-boots and spurs – my silken dalliance – went into the wardrobe, their place being taken by my old school puttees. Though I knew them to be the most time-wasting, vein-constricting form of leg-wear ever devised, they would have to do for the time being.

At Woolwich I had been issued with a Webley .45 revolver. It was heavy and had a powerful kick. A Colt automatic would have been lighter and more to my taste; but we were told at the Shop that nothing less than a .45 bullet would stop a man in his tracks, which seemed a good thing to be able to do; and also that the Germans would shoot out of hand anyone they caught with a quick-firing automatic. I therefore decided to play the game according to the RMA rules – and subsequently wasted quite a lot of energy carrying the Webley around, but never succeeded in killing anyone with it.

My proudest possession was a pair of Zeiss binoculars engraved with the name of Admiral Prince Louis of Battenberg, who had been First Sea Lord up till 1914. My enterprising mother had somehow acquired these second-hand, hoping they might bring me luck. Finally a valise of basic clothing, a pocket bible and a finely bound edition of *Pickwick Papers* completed my kit. The trying moment of family farewells was got over at Edinburgh. Next day, among all the tear-stained faces on the Waterloo platform, my brother's cheerful wave of the hand was the last of it for me.

On the train I met another newly fledged officer from the Shop. At Southampton's South Western Hotel we sat down together to our last meal on English soil, a royal feast of toasted crumpets and blackcurrant jam, followed by strawberries and cream. My companion was in great spirits, quoting *Henry V* as faultlessly as if he had written it himself.

> Now, lords, for France; the enterprise whereof
> Shall be to you as us like glorious.
> We doubt not of a fair and lucky war . . .
>
> For who is he, whose chin is but enriched
> With one appearing hair that will not follow
> These culled and choice-drawn cavaliers to France?

Presently leaning together on the rail of the tubby little steamer SS *Archangel*, we watched Calshot Spit, the Hampshire coast and the Isle of Wight slide away in the gathering darkness.

CHAPTER THREE

Life at the Wagon-Lines

*June 19th, 1917. Written from the Royal Field
Artillery Base Depot, Harfleur*

We had a good crossing, fairly calm and a fitful moon, with
patches of fog. Our hootings should have attracted all the
submarines for miles around, but we were escorted by a
semi-submersible destroyer – a strange fish – and all was
well.

This morning we landed at Havre and explored the
town; quaint houses and innumerable cafés; extraordinary
smells and strange looking folk. Then we trammed out to
the camp at Harfleur, where the rest of the day was spent in
small collapsible huts, in pouring rain, but very cheery. Now
I am writing this by a guttering candle at 10 p.m., lying on
my back on two thicknesses of rug on the boarded floor.
The roll of the valise supports my head, and there are signs
that some parasitic livestock have accompanied me off the
boat. It is difficult to realise that we are in France or that a

war is on. We might be in Camp on Salisbury Plain. Can't hear the guns yet. This address will find me until I am at the front.

June 23rd. On the train to somewhere

This will be a running letter, and I don't know when or where I'll post it. I have been lucky enough to be sent to General Plumer's army, the 2nd, which recently flung back the Huns from Messines Ridge. It's good to think there will be something doing on our part of the line, even though you may not share this sentiment.

I have been given charge of a draft of 35 R.F.A men, who have to be delivered to a certain brigade near railhead. They were issued with bulk rations to last two days, and the corporal in charge said he would look after them. I warned him not to scoff all the grub on the first day. They're not a very smart crowd by Woolwich standards, but they seem to know the ropes, which is more than I do. We had a six-mile march to the station, and after filling up endless forms in the Railway Transport Officer's (R.T.O.) office, I got them entrained by 4 p.m. Having had no food since 6 a.m. breakfast I was glad to buy some from the Station Buffet run, I think, by Lady Angela Forbes. She was awfully decent and gave me a tin of condensed milk as a present. Some other ladies gave us papers from England. I tried to persuade them to come with us, but no luck!

The carriages ranged from our 1st class smoker, with broken windows and a cushion and door missing, to enclosed cattle trucks for the troops. (Hommes 40, chevaux 8.) The enormously long train started at last and reached a speed never more than 20 miles an hour, usually very much less. The Tommies for the most part sat on the steps, dangling their legs and taking a sun bath. For long periods it either stopped or travelled at such a crawl that many passengers got out and walked alongside to stretch their legs along the grass-grown track. Some even had time to visit a wayside estaminet, until recalled by a shriek from the engine, when they emerged at a leisurely speed with arms and pockets crammed with bottles. A lovely sunset and we went to sleep.

As the troops clamoured for dixies of tea from the engine at intervals during the next day, no wonder the poor thing couldn't get up much speed. We skirted Boulogne and Calais and then turning S.E., after innumerable delays, found ourselves at a railhead (Poperinghe) about 6 p.m. The first sign of the front was five observation balloons overlooking the German lines; but still no sound of gunfire. Everything was as peaceful as England; only during the last few hours we had passed several trucks containing captured Boche field-guns, splintered and blackened by shell-fire, and gangs of prisoners in grey uniforms working on the roads.

I got my draft off the train, and suggested a meal; but their two days rations had gone in twenty-four hours! No doubt someone should have been punished for disobeying instructions, but I wasn't looking for trouble. Their unit was said to be at a place 8 miles away, but there was no guide or order for us, and no one knew anything about us. In fact it seemed we were free to start an independent war of our own! Feeling that one war was enough, I left my valise at the station and marched them off. It was not difficult to find the way by map to where their Brigade was said to be stationed, but when we got there at 10 p.m., no sign of the Brigade! Some of the men seemed tired out, probably more accustomed to riding than marching, and for one or two of the feeblest I carried their kit in turn, and tried to cheer them up.

At last a staff officer appeared, and directed us up a by-road. After another mile, some of them being fagged out, I left them by the roadside and went on myself, to search for their unit. Another mile and I met an infantry Major who assured me there were no gunners up that road. It was now dark, and back I went, got the men grumbling to their feet, and off we marched again. Cursing the red-tabbed staff, I felt a bit like Moses leading his people to the promised-land; only these weren't my people and there didn't appear to be a promised land! Meeting another officer, I offered him my beauties as reinforcements, but without success. However another mile beyond the local village we discovered some horse-lines in the darkness, and at last I managed to rouse the sleeping Adjutant, and got the men a shakedown for the night. He was in a bad temper, but I was by then quite reckless and, regardless of rank, told him what I thought of the troop-movement arrangements of his brigade. I then found a corner of a barn, lay down in my trench coat, and was cured of my sulks by the thrilling sight of two Zeppelins over the front to the South East, with searchlights playing on them and the cotton-wool puffs of shells bursting under them. 1 a.m., fell asleep, dead beat.

June 25th. Divisional Ammunition Column, Ouderdom

Here we are in the hamlet of Ouderdom, about 5 miles S.W. of Ypres. What an uncouth name! The Tommies call it Ee-per, Ee-prees, or Wipers; but the officers try to get it into one syllable, like a Hiccup. The rows of limbered ammunition wagons, spotlessly clean, and lines of horses and mules tethered to picketing ropes make a fine sight. At one side near a muddy stream there is a group of bell-tents, and tent shelters for the men, with small marquees serving as officers' mess, sergeants' mess, quartermaster's stores, saddlers', shoeing-smiths' and veterinary sergeant's quarters.

When I reported here, I was shown round by a subaltern, Wilcox by name, a ranker.* The batteries to

* An officer promoted up from the ranks.

which we are to supply ammunition are in a pretty hot spot at the south corner of the Ypres Salient, already known to history as Hill 60. I'm fair panting to see it!

June 26th. D.A.C. Ouderdom

Speaking generally, the officers and men whom I have met are an awfully decent crowd, everyone bent on helping everyone else all he can. It is very different from Woolwich where everyone was intent on spotting faults in other people, and fiercely competing for a high place on the passing-out list. But one elderly ranker here tells me a nasty bit of news – that the expectation of life of a gunner subaltern in the Ypres Salient is three weeks.* I thought he was joking at first, and replied that it hardly seemed worthwhile to come out here. But it appears that he wasn't. It leaves one very little time. This sinking feeling in the stomach must be what a murderer feels when he gets the death sentence, with three weeks to go. And I haven't murdered anyone yet. Well, when I really get to the front, I'll certainly do my best to knock off more than one Boche in the short time at my disposal.

The horses here are a rather scratch lot, and it is surprising to see so many American mules. They are well spoken of as being hardier and less excitable under fire than horses; and, though they are more particular about their drinking water, they can do well on less than the standard ration of 8 lbs. oats and 8 lbs. chaff. I am told they rarely give trouble provided you don't face them and pull at them. The fact that they can kick with their fore legs as well as their hind certainly entitles them to some respect. One enormous mule stands over seventeen hands, is quite black, and

---

* Records show that the turnover of officers in the 112th Brigade, RFA, between October 1915 and December 1917 was just over 100 per cent.

incredibly old, they say. He has a huge hooked nose, and the peculiar conformation of his backbone and withers and his gaunt ribs have earned him the name of 'Vimy Ridge'. He has a proud aloof look in his eye, as if recalling better days and deploring the fate that has made him consort in his declining years with such low company as those around him.

June 27th. 101st D.A.C.

Still here. Nothing seems to happen very fast in this war apparently, and I may be here for a week or two. We spend the morning grooming and watering the horses and are then free till evening stables. Wilcox and I went in to Poperinghe for lunch at the Toc H Club – nice, but crowded. I enjoyed sitting in the garden among the flowers. Life in Pop goes on apparently normally, all shops open and doing a thriving trade. Heard a long-range shell whoop into the town, but it was not near us and no one takes much notice if another house goes up in a cloud of brick-dust. Some quite pretty girls in a lace and handkerchief shop, when asked if they minded the shells, shrugged their shoulders and smiled, '*C'est la guerre!*' With one of them in particular, I would have liked to carry the conversation a great deal further, but there wasn't a hope in all that crowd.

It seems we have a skeleton in the cupboard. I asked Wilcox where our C.O. was – and got the brief answer, 'In his tent.' As I've now been here two days it seemed odd not to have seen him to report to. Our other ranker officer, a decent old Devonshire man, was even more silent. So I went to the C.O.'s tent and looked in. There he was on his bed, a stout elderly man, with purple face and blue lips, unconscious and breathing, as they say, stertorously. I sought out Wilcox and said he seemed to be ill; but he said he was only dead drunk. He gets like this for three or four days on end, apparently, and then the officers and his servant keep it quiet – and to any visitors 'the C.O. is away in Poperinghe'. A bit risky I would have thought. I can't think why he does this; because, when a day later he re-appeared rather groggily (an appropriate word!) and reeking of it, he seemed for all that not a bad chap – a ranker captain. But I kept my distance, and my mouth shut. Perhaps he's had a hard time of it, and this is his way out.

June 30th. Ouderdom, D.A.C.

Still here, and I am getting bored to tears, in spite of a first introduction to shell-fire. This afternoon four shells arrived at one-minute intervals, landing in a farmhouse on the main road about 30 yards from the far end of our horse lines. Woomp! Bits of house, tiles, splinters and brick fragments shot into the air and fell all around us. I was in charge of the watering at the time, and cleared the men away from the dangerous end of the horse lines and sent them over towards our tents. It really was an impressive sight to see the house collapse like a pack of cards. It was being used as a bakery, but was empty at the time. Lucky too that none of our men or horses were hit. These were long-range shells, swooping down from a height of several miles, so fast that the sound of their burst is followed by the noise of their approach. The men called them Silent Susie, Previous Percy, and some less printable names.

About half an hour later – in fact just ten minutes ago – there was a shrieking crash and another shell fell in a field of turnips just across the stream. I have just paced it, and it was 24 yards away. A huge spout of soft earth went up, and some of it came down on me, but no harm was done. Two drivers are over there now in the crater looking for the fuse as a souvenir. They think the Boche is aiming at the railway lines that run about a hundred yards on each side of the camp. Our guns have been giving him hell for some time past, and his aim is too erratic to be quite safe from our point of view. But it's no use to worry, as we can't do anything about it.

*

(Later in the evening)
After I wrote that, we had some more of it. No less than eighteen of them within 300 yards of us, two actually in the wagon-lines, near the water-trough. One smashed a wagon into little pieces. Everyone fell on their faces, but I was too slow and merely retired under a horse-blanket hanging on a rail – an idiotic thing to do, when you come to think of it, but instinctive. I must try not to do it again. Several horses were hit, squealed and kicked, but no other casualties. It was something for the veterinary sergeant to do. The horses didn't seem to mind their flesh wounds once they calmed down; at any rate they only reacted mildly when iodine was rubbed in. We collected some nasty-looking bits of jagged steel, some weighing over a pound, which hummed viciously as they flew through the air. The shells must come from at least 12 miles away, as we are 8 miles behind the lines. What a waste of effort for so little result. A pity some-one can't tell them it's not worth it!

Don't worry about me; I'll be as safe as houses – safer, perhaps!

I have been doing a bit of censoring of the men's letters, a job nobody likes. When reading the letters I never look at their names, so as to be quite impersonal about it. But among this batch I read 'I am simply alive with vermin'. So to him, I had to become personal – and he has been sent straight off to have a carbolic bath.

I have not so far found anything to censor, indeed, I feel more like adding 'hear, hear' to some of the dark threats expressed as to what will happen to highly paid transport and munitions workers now on strike 'when the boys come home'. I've just had a letter of good wishes from little Thatcher, my servant at the Shop, 'hoping you'll excuse the liberty of me writing to an officer'! Such kindness warms the heart; I won't forget him.

There is a little graveyard by our stream, where seven Sikhs lie buried. Each wooden cross carries an aluminium name plate punched out with the name, regiment, date and 'killed in action', early in 1915. Loyalty brought them a long way to lie by this muddy stream. May Allah rest their souls.

July 2nd. Ouderdom, D.A.C.

I was just going to bed last night, when a limber arrived with a subaltern and his kit; and who should it be but my section commander when I was in my second term at the Shop. He shares my tent, and it's a joy to have someone to talk to – especially as our C.O. is again 'indisposed'.

This afternoon I got my first job to do on my own – taking a convoy of G.S. wagons* to load at an ammunition dump. It was not as dull as it sounds. We found the dump all right in the fields a couple of miles towards the line, and were in the middle of loading up with 18-pounder shells, when 'Baron Richthofen's Flying Circus' appeared overhead, five very fast machines painted scarlet and led by Germany's star airman. They circled and dived about the place, while we stood still, keeping our fingers crossed and hoping to escape their attention. The dump was cleverly camouflaged with tarpaulin covers painted to look like a row of country cottages; and soon they moved off southwards, sending two of our observation balloons down in flames as they went. I handed over the loaded wagons to a subaltern who was to take them up to the gun positions.

I later heard they lost three men and a whole wagon team that night, including, alas, poor old Vimy Ridge. When it was hit, the wagon had fortunately been emptied of ammunition or things would have been even worse.

---

* General Service wagons.

July 3rd

Today I took a convoy of fifty-five remount mules north beyond Pop to be dipped for mange. It was just like a sheep-dip, with a gangway taking one horse at a time. But horses, and especially mules, are more suspicious than sheep; so they disarm their suspicions very neatly by first walking the horse through a pool of sheep-dip a mere six inches deep; then round a corner in the gangway and into a similar pool, only this one is five or six feet deep; and as the bottom isn't there when he steps out, he disappears completely in the steaming green scum, reappearing a moment later to flounder up the slope into the hands of his driver. And so home, bedraggled, smelly, but free from infection.

July 4th. With C Battery, 204th Brigade Royal Field Artillery

At last I have left the Divisional Ammunition Column and been transferred to a battery; though so far only to its wagon line, 1½ miles further forward. The country here is quite flat, a maze of fields and hedges intersected by wide ditches lined with stunted willow trees. Everywhere there are infantry encampments and the wagon-lines of batteries whose guns are in action in the forward areas. Tents, huts and marquees, all are camouflaged with branches or splotched with green and brown paint, though I would doubt if they really escape the eyes of the Boche balloons that hang in the sky around the Ypres Salient. The Major of this battery is a great chap, an ex-parson they say, with an incredible flow of lurid language – making up for lost time, no doubt. I live in a bell-tent with camp-bed etc., and also for the first time have a charger of my own, a nice bay mare of fifteen hands.

A warm evening in more ways than one! We had just finished supper in our shirt sleeves when – CRASH! A huge shell burst on the parade ground. I ducked so hard that my chin hit the table. At once the Major went into action, yelling his commands; and in less than five minutes the wagon-lines were deserted, the entire battery of horses and men having moved into another field well off the line of fire. More of these great thunderbolts slammed down on the horse-lines about once a minute, each explosion being greeted with jeers by the men watching from the safety of the side-lines. After a quarter of an hour, there was a pause; and I was sent round the billets to see that everyone was clear. It didn't take long to find that out. There were huge craters here and there, with clods of turf all over the place. One crater was at the door of my tent, of which only the poles and some torn canvas survived. But my gear, which had been on the ground, was quite undamaged. On the ground seems the best place to be.

After a while more shells came over every half-hour or so, just enough to make us spend part of the night in the open. I lay with the others under the lee of a hedge, with the end of a rein around my hand. The mare stood quiet as a lamb, and I managed to get some sleep. Why have I never spent a night in the open before? And such a perfect night it was. With my head pillowed in my tin hat, gazing up at the dark star-spangled sky, the earth was soon left far behind, and I was up there floating in the great silences of the Milky Way and looking to see if Orion's sword-belt was properly buckled. Under the gaze of the witnessing stars how insignificant become our human antics, our quarrels, even our wars. If we choose to blow ourselves to pieces they will not waver an inch in their vast orbits . . .

We hear that yesterday the King, the Prince of Wales, and Sir Douglas Haig passed within two miles of here on a tour of inspection; but we missed them, worse luck.

People say the Boche airmen can do pretty well what they like round here. Of course our long line of observation balloons are sitting ducks for the Boche. This morning the sound of a low-flying aeroplane made me look up just in time to see one, with sinister black crosses on its wings, dive out of a low cloud at a balloon only about a mile away from here. The short rattle of machine-gun fire reached us as it zoomed up into the clouds again. A moment later a spurt of flame appeared and the stricken balloon crumpled, while two parachutes fluttered out below and drifted sideways on the wind. In a matter of seconds all that remained was a ball of fire falling steadily to leave a great exclamation mark of smoke in the sky.

We laughed, rather heartlessly, to see two more balloon crews abandon ship in expectation of being shot up next. But the Boche must have seen some of our planes, as he suddenly cleared off. The empty balloons were wound down, and the spectacle was at an end.

Several days ago two R.F.C.* men were up in a sausage right here above our wagon-line when a Boche airman strafed[†] them. They jumped, and their parachutes opened all right, but it was dead calm, and the burning balloon caught them up, set their parachutes alight, and the whole lot fell through the roof of some nearby stables and burnt two horses as well.

* Royal Flying Corps, predecessor of the Royal Air Force.
[†] 'Strafe' = Punish. This expressive word was gratefully adopted from the German slogan 'Gott strafe England!'

CHAPTER FOUR

Death on Hill 60

July 8th, 1917. A Battery, 112th Brigade R.F.A.
Another change of unit. It seems that G.H.Q. can't make up their minds whether to make me the spear-head of their next attack, or to hide me away where I can do least harm. More probably my movements are those of a leaf, blown by the wind of chance. But at least it has blown me into the Front Line and out again.

On the night of 6th, an officer of C Battery, 204 Brigade, was taking a column of forty-eight pack mules, each with eight rounds of 18 pdr. ammunition, to the gun position on Hill 60; and I was sent up with him. We set off in the dusk and reached Dickebusch Lake by the time the moon was up. Despite its idyllic name, no dicky birds sang in that bush. An eerie silence brooded over the dark lake and its surrounding woods. But every five minutes or so some 60-pounders (the noisiest guns we have) flashed out and shattered the peaceful night as their shells roared away into the darkness.

At the Café Belge Crossroads, the ruined buildings had been strengthened with sandbags to form a dressing-station. The red triangle of the Y.M.C.A. hung out next door and, as we rode by, we got a glimpse of flags and bright lights inside. A group of mud-caked Jocks, their legs stockinged with sandbags, stood at the counter sipping hot coffee in an attempt to drive the clammy chill of the mud from their weary limbs.

Further on as we left the road the trees thinned out; their broken boughs hung down with withered leaves, and before long we were in a region where the few remaining trees, now merely gaunt and blackened skeletons, raised their splintered arms as if in protesting agony. Here the ground was pitted with huge waterlogged shell craters, in which the moon shone with ghostly beauty. Silently and slowly we took our way along the winding track through that desolate morass, men and pack-mules in single file, strange visitants to a lunar landscape. And I found running through my head that melancholy verse

> O what can ail thee, knight-at-arms,
> Alone and palely loitering?
> The sedge has withered from the lake,
> And no birds sing.

I hope no one could say 'I see a lily on thy brow'; though to tell the truth, for a first-timer, it didn't need La Belle Dame Sans Merci to put it there.

Several shell bursts broke the peace of Convent Lane without harming us. Presently we came to cross the Yser Canal by a small wooden bridge at a place called Spoil Bank, and I could tell by the whispering that those who knew the spot would be glad when they had passed it. There was a general uneasiness in the column like that of a horse smelling blood. Dead horses, swollen to bursting, lay around among the splintered remnants of ammunition wagons; but our stolid mules kept on their way. It was a lucky night for us; we got safely across and were soon making our way over the lower slopes of Hill 60 towards the gun position.

While the mules were being unloaded several rounds of shrapnel burst so close that we almost thought it was aimed, though I suppose they could not have known we were there. Presently the convoy returned for home; and Captain Cross, who is in charge of the Battery, took me down blinking into the light of the Officers' Mess Dug-out.

I had the top bunk to sleep in, and the white-painted iron roof was just a foot above my head. Barely had we turned in when a steady bombardment of five-nines and four-point-twos opened on the gun position. The dug-out shook, and trickles of sand and gravel fell out of the sand-bag walls. I would have given a lot to know whether our roof would stand a direct hit, but as the answer would no doubt have been 'Wait and see,' it seemed not a good moment to ask.

The crashing and thudding went on for over an hour. Then the Captain put his head out to have a look round, couldn't see anything, and got through to Brigade H.Q. on the 'phone to ask for some counter-battery retaliation. Whether as the result or not, the shelling presently ceased. After a while he rang the battery exchange to find out if they had any news. No reply. We both went round to the telephonists' dug-out. It was empty. One corner of it had been smashed in, but the lines were undamaged and were plugged through to Brigade. Telling me to return to the Mess, the Captain disappeared down a mine shaft, where he presently found the telephonists and ordered them back to the Exchange. Faint echoes of King's Regulations came into my mind, about the dire penalty for abandoning one's post in the face of the enemy. But as the Captain made no further comment, I gather that King's, and most other, Regulations can become quite elastic out here.

The morning brought further insight into the situation. The battery had been there more than a fortnight and was one of a number of silent batteries which would only start firing when the big Push would begin. Till then its job was to remain concealed and inactive. Captain Cross showed me the guns almost buried in a hedge, and took me down the mine-shaft, where I saw twenty or thirty men sitting dejectedly in a long lamp-lit corridor that smelt horribly of stale sweat and sandbags. There, it seems, they sat in the same half-gloom by day and night – playing cards, reading and sleeping, or just sitting. There was some talk of last night's shelling, and I got the impression that safety loomed rather large in their minds, and that they were not in any hurry to come up into the daylight. It all seemed an unhappy situation, and I thought it best not to ask questions about it.

After breakfast, Captain Cross announced, 'Come on, young feller, I'll take you round the front line.' And off we went. The ground round the battery was churned up with last night's shelling, and it was surprising that no serious damage was done. Looking to the north, less than two miles away, we could see among the bare trees the ramparts and ruins of Ypres – and to the south-east the summit of the low hill with the historic name, Hill 60, whose tenure has cost so many lives on both sides. Little more than a mile to the South lay the north end of the Messines Ridge, scarred brown from the eruption of huge land-mines just a month ago.

The sun was hot as we took our way along a field track, where poppies and marguerites still grow by the wayside. A little ahead a khaki figure could be seen asleep against the bank. It seemed an odd place to choose for a siesta, barely a mile from the enemy trenches; but there he was, a rather stout man with a very dark complexion. As we came up to

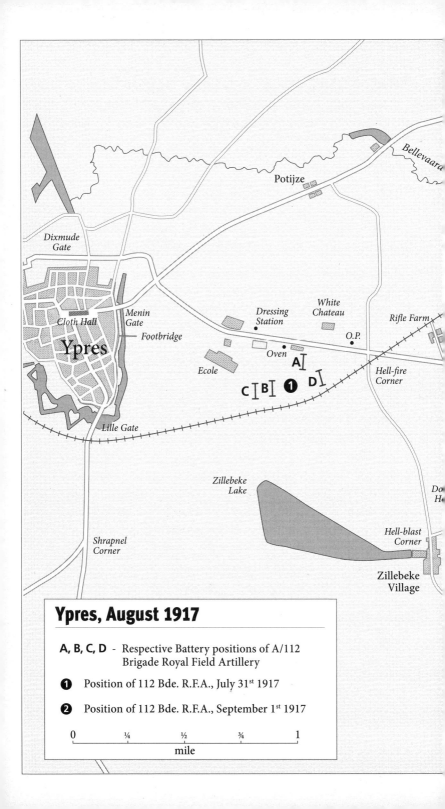

Bellevaarde

Potijze

Dixmude
Gate

White
Chateau

Dressing
Station

Rifle Farm

Menin
Gate

Cloth Hall

Footbridge

O.P.

Ypres

Oven

A

Ecole

C [B] ❶ D [

Hell-fire
Corner

Lille Gate

Zillebeke
Lake

Do
H

Hell-blast
Corner

Shrapnel
Corner

Zillebeke
Village

Ypres, August 1917

A, B, C, D - Respective Battery positions of A/112
Brigade Royal Field Artillery

❶ Position of 112 Bde. R.F.A., July 31st 1917

❷ Position of 112 Bde. R.F.A., September 1st 1917

| 0 | ¼ | ½ | ¾ | 1 |

mile

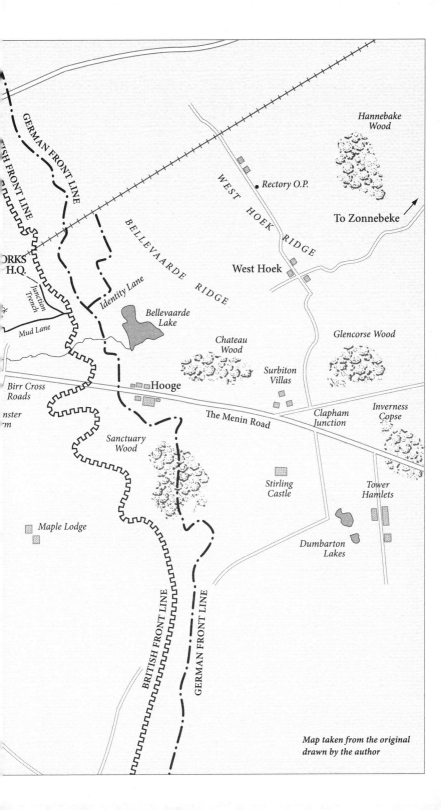

Map taken from the original
drawn by the author

him, two bluebottles crawled slowly from his nostrils, and I realised with a shock that he was very dead. I have never seen anyone dead before, and I could hardly take my eyes off him.

Again the questions crowded into one's mind. How had he died? A glance as we passed by revealed no obvious injury. Who was he? Didn't anyone know about it? The Captain appeared quite uninterested; so I asked him, 'Why doesn't someone bury him? Surely he can't just be left there?' 'This isn't a very healthy spot,' was all he replied, 'unless you keep moving.' We continued on our way, with me wondering just how unhealthy it might be, and how soon our walk towards the enemy might take us below ground level.

Presently we passed the smashed remains of a wagon and four decayed horses (phew!), went through the ruins of Zillebeke Village and, near Hell-blast Corner, entered a long shallow communication trench, sign-posted 'Wellington Crescent'. The German field-guns were searching the area. Their shells, so aptly named 'whizz-bangs', made us duck as the fragments of jagged steel whizzed past. I thought of Larkhill and the three rounds we were allowed to fire there. Here my education was being carried a stage further by see-ing field-gun shells burst at close quarters. But the lesson was rather longer than it need have been, and I was glad when we turned up an alley and passed through a low door-way into a large heap of brick rubble, which was the Dormy House O.P. (Observation Post). Here through a concrete slot I had my first long look through binoculars at the enemy trenches. The gunner subaltern on duty pointed out the various landmarks which were not easy to see in that monotonous landscape.

First there was the area of Sanctuary Wood; not really a wood, only a wilderness of splintered tree-stumps, and certainly no place to go for sanctuary. Stirling Castle, a long grey stone mound. As I watched, a shell droned overhead and burst on it, raising a great mushroom of dust into the air. It drifted away, leaving the mound apparently unaffected.

Then over to the left, more skeleton trees, identified as Glencorse Wood, Inverness Copse, and Blackwatch Corner. Easy to see the Jocks had left their mark on this piece of Belgium. Other names too spoke of those who had passed this way. Tower Hamlets, Clapham Junction and Surbiton Villas told of the Cockney and the suburban resident; Maple Lodge of the Canadians; Leinster Farm of the Irish. But don't think that these places could be identified by anyone but an expert. All I could see was lines and lines of sandbags alternating with hedges of rusty barbed wire, brown earth and grey splintered tree-trunks.

The map showed that, through all this, a streamlet called the Bassevillebeek trickled out of a couple of ponds, marked Dumbarton Lakes; and becoming suddenly informative, it also recorded 'steep banks, marshy bottom 2 ft. deep, obstacle to Cavalry'. I must say the idea of cavalry had not occurred to me in this context. And the thought that the Ordnance people might have a sense of humour became a certainty when I read in a footnote to my map, 'The fact that an obstacle is not represented on the map does not necessarily mean that there is none there'! Physical obstacles were visible in plenty, thickets of tangled wire and undergrowth; and no doubt plenty of machine-gun bullets for anyone who was rash enough to show himself. The most striking thing was the absence of all movement, or of any sign of the enemy; and the brooding silence, broken only by the occasional burst of a shell.

We went further and reached our very front trench. Here I was given a periscope and, raising it gingerly over the top, at last looked the Boche in the face. Nothing to be seen. Only more sandbags, bushes and long grass in no-man's-land; and rusty wire, belts and belts of it like withered bracken; and not far away the tattered remains of someone who had died on the wire in some night encounter. The smell of chloride of lime hung heavy in the air mingling with the stench of corpses and latrines. Drowsy bluebottles buzzed and swarmed on the wooden framework of the trenches.

Most of the infantry sat in small shelters excavated in the face of the trench. They were relaxed, even bored, for the wire ruled out an enemy attack during daylight. Presently however there was an explosion in our lines, and the word went round – 'Look out, Minnies!' 'There's one,' said a sergeant, pointing upwards. I looked up and saw a black object about the size of a small pig turning slowly over as it reached the top of its trajectory and began to fall towards our lines. Down it came, a couple of hundred yards away, with an earth-shaking explosion and a cloud of black smoke. There is something fatal and inescapable about the Minnie (Minenwerfer, I believe, if you speak the language). And no wonder the front-line infantryman hates them more than anything else.

I asked the Sergeant about this. But he said things might be worse. They were fairly safe below ground level, as shells didn't often fall into the trench; and they were only there for two or three days at a time, then two or three days in the support line; and after that back into reserve for a week or more out of harm's way. In fact, he preferred that to the gunner's life, moving around in the open all day with a Boche in a sausage balloon watching for a good chance to knock you off, and no chance of a quiet evening in an estaminet for weeks on end.

Before leaving we watched a small shoot by our 6 inch howitzers. For five minutes shell after shell shrieked over and burst on a redoubt in the Boche line. What appeared to be sandbags and other debris shot into the air, out of a cloud of shell-smoke and dust. Then silence reigned again, and the bluebottles buzzed and droned in the hot sunshine.

In the afternoon, back at the battery position, we saw a thrilling air fight, five of ours versus seven Boches. They twisted and turned overhead, machine-gunning each other, until one of our machines came spinning down out of control. On the way down it burst into flames, and we saw the pilot and observer fall out at about 1,000 feet up, and turning over and over come straight down to earth, and the machine on top of them. They fell only 300 yards in front of the battery, and we ran over but could not get near owing to the flames. Anyway they must both have been killed by the fall. I wonder why they didn't have parachutes like the balloon boys?*

The Captain has had a message that I am to be transferred. He tells me that the General commanding this division wants his nephew brought out of the 25th Division to be his orderly officer. In exchange, the 25th are to receive his last joined artillery Subaltern, namely me. They say the 25th is a fine division; it was on the Somme and in the centre of the Messines show. I am secretly rather glad, because they don't seem a very happy lot here. I am due to leave tomorrow morning.

At dusk we had a real shindy. Machine-gun fire started furiously in the trenches – a raid, I suppose – S.O.S.† rockets went up, green and silver, and lovely to watch (from a distance). Then the guns on both sides (except this silent battery of course) opened up and started a hell of a row. Out in the open it was difficult, short of shouting in a person's ear, to make anyone hear at all. Then a few shells burst very

---

* The reason was that early parachutes were too bulky for the constricted cockpits of aircraft, but could be worn in balloon baskets.
† The emergency call for help, which gunners answer at once, regardless.

near us, and one of them caught a small-arms ammunition dump. This went on fire, and bullets exploded in all directions; so we retired into our dug-out, and hoped that the fire would not reach a dump of heavy trench mortars close by. During the night the fire burnt itself out, but not before it had attracted more shelling at intervals from the Boche. The hellish noise went on till long after midnight, and left me with a real headache. Not a wink of sleep all night.

Just before dawn today a ration cart arrived, and I slung in my valise, said goodbye to Captain Cross, and mounted the horse that my relief officer had ridden.

We returned by the same route, with the rising sun behind us, and occasional shells searching the back areas.

Just as we reached Dickebusch village a long range shell swooped into it. I made the party halt, and sure enough a minute later another one arrived; whereupon we cantered through at a smart pace that almost rattled the bolts out of the ration cart, and had just got clear when two more crashed into the ruined houses. My horse was even keener than I to get back from the front line, and I have a large blister on my finger through trying to hold him in.

A broiling hot morning, and breakfast out in the sunshine. Now I have only to say goodbye to the Major, and walk over to the 25th Divisional Artillery whose wagon-lines are a bare half mile away; and then to start afresh with them, this time I hope for keeps.

CHAPTER FIVE

Feeding the Guns

July 12th, 1917. A Battery, 112th Brigade R.F.A.
It's four days now since I joined the 25th Div. Artillery. They seem a very good crowd, and most of the officers awfully nice. Their tails are well up, as a result of the Messines Show. They say it went like clockwork from A to Z, and delighted everyone from General Plumer down to the front line troops, not least the lucky man whose job it was to touch off the Spanbrookmolen Mine, the largest of nineteen – a hundred and fifty yards across. It must have been the biggest bang of all time.*

Our wagon-lines are a mile and a half north west of where I first was, in exactly the same flat agricultural ditchy country. The guns too are north of Hill 60, i.e. right in front of Ypres, just about the hottest spot in the salient. It can be

---

* The blast was so enormous that the tremor was said to have been felt in Downing Street, 130 miles away.

no secret to the Boche that he's going to get a bloody nose here; our guns are at him day and night, flattening out the wire in front of his trenches, and generally make his life a burden behind them. So we are pretty busy taking ammunition up to the guns. This can only be done in the dark because he can see everything that moves in the salient by day – and he doesn't approve of movement! In fact his aeroplanes come over and photograph us away back here – and that accounts for occasional long-range shells on anything he thinks wasn't there before. We are, as the estate agents say, in a pleasantly rural situation, in a big hayfield with the officers' tents etc under some trees. But when it rains the landscape becomes depressing to look at, and we slither about in the mud.

Two nights ago, Captain Jones gave me my first responsible job – to try me out, I think – taking up nineteen limbered wagons of ammunition and a G.S. wagon of supplies to the gun position in front of Ypres. It sounds easy enough; but I had never been over the route by daylight, let alone in the dark, and part of the route lay across open country to a battery position which is just a map reference point. Already I have learned that, near the line, as a result of persistent shelling maps can be misleading. Things are usually not what they ought to be, and are probably no longer where the map says they are; and on a dark night you wouldn't see them if they were! However there were two good sergeants under me, and it was largely thanks to them that we all got back in one piece.

We were due to leave at the ghastly hour of 1 a.m. At half past midnight my batman's efforts to wake me were at last successful and, after a cup of tea and a sandwich, I scrambled into my clothes and peeped outside the tent. A pale bleary moon looked down through scudding clouds, and in the distance twinkles of flame and heavy thuds showed where the Hun bird was dropping its eggs. I strapped my revolver and the new leather torch to my belt, put cigarettes and map in one pocket, and a field-dressing and compass in the other, fixed my box-respirator on my chest, crowned the whole with a tin-hat, stepped out of the tent, and promptly went base-over-apex over a tent-rope. Scraping the mud off my hands and knees I mounted my horse, greeted the senior sergeant, who reported the column ready to move; and off we went to the ammunition dump. Loading in the dark took time, as the only light allowed was from dim lanterns, but at last it was finished. I signed the receipt and led the convoy out on to the road in the direction of Ypres.

We had not gone very far before we were in a traffic block, held up by the traffic control men, who said there was heavy shelling on the road a couple of miles ahead – as indeed we could hear. This went on for half an hour. If only the Boche had had the sense to search down the road westwards, he could have wiped us out. But he didn't. When we eventually reached the point, he was still at it, but the shells were whistling and crashing into a field to one side.

By this time the night had darkened, and rain was falling. On every side were flashes and explosions which made one fairly jump. Some may have been bursting shells, others no doubt were the discharge of our heavy guns, 8 inch and 9.2 inch howitzers, pounding the enemy trenches from long range; but as I couldn't tell which was which, the effect was twice as frightening as it need have been. My horse behaved fairly well however, and I was able to get a glimpse of the map by the light of my new torch.

We were at a place called Belgian Battery Corner, a road intersection that was no doubt a safe bet for the Boche gunners when strafing the back areas. In fact I had been told that some nights before, another ammunition convoy from our brigade had been badly shot up there, and lost many horses and several men. The officer in charge had been given an M.C. – for being first off his horse and into the ditch, so they said. I gathered he was more popular with his battery commander than with the officers and men.

Further on, we turned off on to a 'corduroy track', made of wooden logs laid crosswise on the muddy fields. They proved to be slippery and many of the lead horses stumbled, but at least there was no risk of being stuck in deep mud. Suddenly we became aware of a strong smell of gas. But as there was some wind, it was too dispersed to be dangerous and we didn't have to add to our difficulties by putting on gas masks. Presently we crossed the Yser Canal and reached 'Shrapnel Corner'.

The chap who decided on the names of these places must have had a morbid mind. It's easy enough to get the wind up without the map making your flesh creep with such names as Hell-Fire, Hell-Blast, and Shrapnel Corner. The lunar-cratered landscape, with its tortured trees, flooded shell-holes, and putrefying carcasses of horses among tangles of barbed wire, seen by the fitful light of the moon on a blustery rainy night, surely this is enough without the implication that shrapnel may be expected to burst over you at any minute. Now if only they had called it Sunny Bank, Bluebell Corner – or since we are in a foreign land – Sans Souci or Mon Repos, I for one would find it a little more reassuring. Though admittedly a dead horse smells the same in any language. At that particular moment, however, there was no shrapnel; and I led on through the darkness towards the Lille Gate, thankful to find we had not yet lost our way.

It was quite a thrill to come at last to this famous mediaeval city, the core of the notorious Ypres Salient, the city that has already given its unpronounceable name to two battles in this war and, for all I know, looks like giving it to a third. There was a moonlight glimpse of two gateway towers, and a bridge over a wide moat, as we turned off the road and struck out eastwards towards the battery position in front of the city.

It was 3 a.m. and in spite of delays we were well on time. Sergeant White rode up alongside to report that we were all close up in one column, and all was well. He knew exactly where the gun-pits were, and where the limbered wagons could best pull up; so I let him get on with it.

Our arrival was greeted with shouts; and presently lanterns and torches flickered in the darkness. In no time at all gunners appeared and formed chains to pass the shells rapidly from hand to hand between the wagons and the gun-pits. Seeing the job well under way I called to Sergeant White telling him to form the wagons up in two lines when they had unloaded, and let me know when they were ready to start the homeward trip; meanwhile I would report to the battery commander. The sergeant-major loomed up out of the darkness and led me to the officers' mess dugout; I went down some steps into an underground cellar, pulled back the gas blanket in the doorway, saluted and reported our arrival.

My new C.O. was seated in shirt and breeches on a stretcher; he had fair curly hair and looked quite young. With a glass of whisky in one hand, he adjusted a monocle with the other and glared at me through it. 'Who the hell are you?' he demanded rather fiercely; and then, having run his eye over me, said, 'Well, at any rate you're on time. This your first trip up?' When I admitted this, he thawed a bit, and was soon almost friendly. He had been at the guns supervising a shoot most of the night. Little wonder that he was somewhat peevish at being interrupted when at last he got to bed. But he poured out a stiff glass of whisky and handed it to me.

'No thank you, Sir,' I said. He looked at me blankly.

'I'm sorry Sir, I don't like it.'

'Sounds bloody silly to me,' he remarked severely.

'Well, I promised my people,' I explained rather lamely.

'Well, that's different, I suppose,' he said; and went on to question me about the training I had had. It seemed that my credentials from Woolwich might go some way to atone for my eccentricity in regard to whisky.

As we talked I looked around the dugout that might soon be my home. On the table was a whisky bottle with a candle stuck in it; but the main light came from an acetylene lamp that, hissing faintly, shed an ashen light all around. Apart from the central table, the rest of the furniture consisted of packing-cases and stretchers – on one of which a subaltern lay snoring rhythmically. There was a Decca Gramophone and a box of records; a large map-board of the battle zone, a case of whisky and a mass of papers and air-photographs. Mackintoshes, gas masks and tin-hats hung from nails in the wall.

From 4 a.m. to 6 a.m., things are usually quiet, but this time some shells could be heard crumping away – and not far off either. Presently the battery sergeant major and Sgt. White came in, with the delivery note for signature, to say that unloading was complete; so we left, with a cheerful 'See you soon I expect', from the Major.

When we reached the gun position, however, only two limbered wagons remained, with a driver holding our horses. In answer to my rather angry question 'Where are all the rest?' Sgt. White, with a blank look on his face replied, 'I don't know, sir. Perhaps they've gone home.' I was furious. What sort of a way was this to march, if the men drove off whenever they felt like it? The odds were they would lose their way in the dark, and a pretty fool I would look reporting at the wagon-line that I had lost my convoy! It was still dark, raining and blowing, and the shelling was getting worse; crumps were dropping at random all over the place. So I led the two remaining wagons back to the Lille Gate, and turned south along the pavé road towards Shrapnel Corner.

Then we got it. Big shells started bursting in the fields along the roadside. We broke into a trot, and followed an empty G.S. wagon whose driver was urging his horses on at a good speed. In the darkness, we couldn't be sure that we had reached Shrapnel Corner, and when suddenly I saw a turning on the right I took it hopefully. But we hadn't gone two hundred yards when it was obvious we were on the wrong road. Worse still, we finished up a narrow lane, on a raised banking facing a barbed wire barricade with no space to turn in. Buffeted by the concussion of the shells, we all set to work unhitching six pairs of horses, heaving the wagons round by hand, and hitching the teams in again. At last it was done, and we were back in the saddle with nothing worse than a nasty gash on the neck of one of the horses, from which blood oozed down its shoulder to its leg.

Back on the main road, along to Shrapnel Corner, turn right again – and off home at a round gallop with the shells shrieking and crashing behind us. At this point, my sense of locality being rather shaken, I began to wonder whether by any chance our nightmare ride wasn't taking us eastwards towards the front line. Reading a compass with a torch, while cantering along a rough road under shell-fire, was at least as difficult as our Woolwich circus act of 'vaulting on and off on the near side'. However the glimpse I managed to get was enough to show that we were travelling roughly westward, a fact soon borne out by seeing over my shoulder the first streak of dawn in an angry sky. But was ever a compass reading taken so inaccurately or noted with such relief!

After that the way home was uneventful. I spent most of the time wondering what would happen when I returned to announce the loss of eighteen out of the twenty wagons entrusted to me. It was unpleasantly like the performance of General Cope after the battle of Prestonpans, when he rode non-stop to Berwick bringing the first news of his own defeat.

When we reached the wagon-lines, all was quiet. Sgt. White went off to see if any of the wagons had got back, and I had a wash and a rest and then breakfast. Fearing the worse, I went on to morning parade. And there they all were, just as if none of them had spent the night on the road! No one gave any explanation. I asked no questions of Sgt. White. And when the captain later asked how things had gone, I just said 'Fine, Sir, thanks.' The fact was that they'd all been up the line before, and knew better than to obey my instructions to wait at the battery position. And as for getting home on their own in the dark, they made a better job of it than I did.

July 14th. A/112 Bde. R.F.A.

Nowadays there seems to be a lot more going on overhead. Richthofen's Circus is often embroiled in dog-fights with our chaps. I'm getting to be able to recognise the aeroplanes on both sides; their Albatrosses and Fokkers with black crosses on their wings, our D.H.4s with staggered upper wing, and the new Sopwith Triplane. My favourite is the Sopwith Camel. But why choose the name of 'Camel' – clumsy and slow – for the neatest machine of all? Anyway it's thrilling to see them roaring low over the fields and banking away with such incredible speed.

Our Archies* are just a joke. When any Boche plane comes over, the white puffs of Archie shells follow it round the sky, usually in double line, and always well behind the plane. Even if they ever succeed in getting a burst in front, it must be at the wrong height, because they hardly ever turn the plane from its course and certainly never bring it down. We field-gunners jeer at them, but when you come to think of it they've got an impossible task, and the most they can hope to do is to put the wind up the Boche pilots.

* Anti-aircraft guns.

Less of a joke is the bombing of our back areas by night. Every now and then a Boche plane appears like a silver gnat in the searchlights and streams of tracer bullets fly up from below – but they never reach their target, and he goes on his way, leaving our chaps to shoot their badly wounded horses, and restore order among the rest. Our battery lines have escaped so far, touch wood, but it does mean broken nights, and some units are putting low sand-bag walls round their tents. On such occasions mother earth may seem more comfortable than a camp bed that is level with the sandbag wall!

There's a bit of a hate on against the Boche pilots for another reason. I've twice seen them, after shooting up our balloons, circle round and machine-gun the observers as they hang from their parachutes. They haven't a chance and can't even try to retaliate. We've even fired rifles at the Boche in the hope that an odd bullet might chance to hit his petrol tank, but no luck so far.

I've been able to choose a charger for myself from some remounts that have just arrived – a very nice little bay mare called Molly; seems to have a good temperament. Two other subalterns and I have rigged up a couple of brushwood jumps 3 or 4 ft high, where we have good fun. I rode into Poperinghe this morning and bought a pair of leather lace-up riding boots. They look good on a horse and will be useful for walking through mud, if necessary. And I'll never wear puttees no more.

I am gradually getting to know some of the N.C.O.s. The 25th Division were volunteers of Kitchener's Army, and first came out in September 1915. As they were all raised and trained together, artillery as well as infantry, they had a wonderful spirit. This still remains in spite of the changes of eighteen months' casualties. They came from the Midland Counties, Worcestershire, Cheshire, Lancashire, Wiltshire and Staffordshire, counties which I know nothing about;

and it is sometimes difficult for me to make out what a man is saying. Being Woolwich trained, a Scot, and raw in the ways of the Western Front doesn't make it any easier. I must seem rather an odd fish to them. But there is no doubt the 25th is one of our crack Divisions, what the Boche calls 'storm-troops', and I am proud to wear the Red Horseshoe Divisional sign on the back of my tunic, whatever the differences underneath. We are to be with two other famous divisions (8th and the Highland 51st) in the centre of the coming offensive.

I hear that last night the Hun sent over a new gas round the gun position. It makes you sneeze and sneeze, and by the time your gas helmet is on you've lost your sense of smell for a while. He then sends over chlorine gas. After a while, people try a sniff, can't detect anything, take off their masks, and the next thing they know is they're choking with chlorine without having suspected its presence. The Hun is a cute devil. But I've bought a tiny bottle of Eau-de-Cologne, and if I run into sneezing gas I won't take my mask off till I can smell the Eau-de-Cologne again. But how complicated life becomes! They say that the new gas can blind you if you get too much of it. Two men at the battery position seem to have lost their sight, poor devils.

July 18th, A/112 Bde./R.F.A.
Two days ago I got orders to take ammunition up to the gun position, and stay a day there to cover the job of an officer who had been killed. The convoy was to be a dozen wagons, and this time we were to go through the centre of Ypres and the Menin Gate.

We loaded up about 11 p.m. and joined the main stream of traffic; very dense; G.S. wagons, ambulances, lorries, water-carts, buses full of infantry, guns, everything imaginable. This time we went by Vlamertinghe, Goldfish Chateau and the Asylum, which some wags among our drivers hailed as an appropriate destination. From the increased traffic on the road, and the amount of guns, equipment and bivouacs in the fields, it's obvious that we are building up for something big; and well the Boche know it, for they have been intensifying their gassing and shelling by night as well as by day.

Our 6 inch, 8 inch and 9.2 inch Howitzers were firing steadily; a good many Boche crumps were coming over. The gun-flashes and explosions in the half-dark made one jumpy. Suddenly a shell shrieked overhead and hit the roadside with a blinding flash. Horses screamed – men shouted. I swung my charger round, and spurring her past rearing horses and panicking wagon-teams, came on a bloody shambles of horses and men by the roadside. Already the three drivers were being dragged out. By a miracle each was only slightly wounded. Two horses torn apart by shell splinters lay twitching convulsively. A third lay with a shattered hind-leg, at which it kept looking round with staring eyes, as it tried to get up off the roadway.

Sergeant Wood, appearing at my shoulder, said, 'Best shoot 'im, Sir.' I put my revolver to its forehead and pulled the trigger. The poor brute groaned, shuddered and collapsed. Then we looked the other three horses over. They were badly gashed, but not beyond recovery.

By this time some officers and men had run across to us; they took the three drivers to a nearby First Aid Station, while a gunner officer and some men helped to drag the three corpses into the shell crater, and led away our three wounded horses. No serious damage had been done to the wagon and its load, so a 4-horse team was quickly made up by two pairs from other teams, and before long things were straightened out.

'Everything all right, Sergeant Wood?' I asked.

'Everything all right, Sir,' he replied.

'Walk, march,' I shouted; and we were on our way.

Thank God the shell fell in the ditch and the burst only affected one wagon team. If it had struck the pavé, well—!

Next we ran into a nasty belt of gas. All respirators had to go on, which made it difficult to see where we were going, except to follow the vehicle in front. This went on for half an hour till we reached the western entrance of Ypres, when the gas cleared away before a light wind. 'You'll be careful, sir, going through,' said the man on point duty, 'six thousand gas shells in tonight, and it's still hanging about.'

As we entered the streets, the moon came out from behind the clouds, and the ruins of this ghostly city took on a strange beauty. In the narrow streets leading to the square several houses were still standing. The front of one had collapsed revealing its interior like a doll's house; wallpaper hanging in strips, an iron bedstead with the remnants of bedclothes and mattress, even a picture askew on the wall; somebody's home wrecked and nothing left. The basement doorway bore a chalked notice 'Rat Villa'.

Presently we reached the Square, where stands the famous Cloth Hall. I've heard of the Taj Mahal by moonlight – but for me it could never be so impressive as this ruin. The stones and masonry gleamed snowy white and the massive tower stood there, raising its jagged turrets against the dark sky like some huge iceberg. Its base emerged from a vast heap of fallen masonry that had been brought down from above, and levelled off into a sea of brick and stone rubble all around the cobbled square. There it stood, the shattered but invincible emblem of all that the Ypres Salient means – awe-inspiring and unforgettable. There was just time to notice by the stump of a lamp post the crumpled body of a dead soldier. Then I had to get busy as we passed on towards the Menin Gate.

For sheer concentrated shelling the Menin Gate stands alone. There is of course no gate there, merely a gap in the stone ramparts of the town, and a causeway crossing the wide moat beyond. Most of the traffic supplying the line in front of Ypres must pass through here, and the Boche takes heavy toll of it – day and night. The bridge, whether originally arched or not, is now a solid mass of stonework, supplemented, indeed cemented, by the remains of smashed vehicles and the fragmented bodies of horses and men. In fact everything that passes over it has contributed to its upkeep. During lulls in the shelling, men dash out from their shelters on the massive ramparts, and patch the holes in the road as best they can.

I ordered the front limber to set off at a canter, and the others to follow at hundred yard intervals, praying that we should win this game of 'tip and run'. We did; and thankful I was when the last wagon swerved round a big shell-hole, rattled across the causeway and out into the country beyond, leaving the sinister gateway behind.

Our way led along the Menin Road through a ghostly desolation of water-logged shell holes and splintered tree stumps. After passing a large ramshackle ruin marked 'Ecole' on the right, Sgt. Wood led the way into a field in front of a ruined white villa, whose cellars constitute the Officers' Mess. The gunners were ready, under the Battery Sergeant-Major, and soon our precious cargo was being unloaded into the gun-pits and other protected ammunition dumps.

The B.S.M. told me they were not doing a shoot until the morning, and the officers were trying to get some sleep. So to avoid disturbing them I searched with my torch among the nearby ruins, and came across a convenient look-ing bread-oven at the side of a house overlooking the battery-position. The door was missing but it had an arched brick roof which looked strong – and a 6 ft. long shelf which would just take a stretcher with me on it. Then arose a problem. Should I sleep with my feet at the open end to protect my head from flying shell-splinters and whiffs of gas, or my head at the open end to minimise the chance of being buried alive by a direct hit? I chose the latter alternative, lay down with my gas mask half on, said a prayer that I might be preserved from 'things that go bump in the night' – and shut my eyes.

But sleep was slow to come. Every now and then a shell burst some distance off. I could hear others like lost souls whimpering their way overhead for some remoter destination. And I realised that at that very moment a German gun might have fired the shell that in half a minute would crash through my oven roof and mangle me like those horses. The thought was so appalling that for the sake of sanity I shut it out from my mind.

This would be my lot in the days to come, to live under sentence of sudden death, yet somehow to ignore it. Men of older years and longer war experience would be looking to me, their officer, for an example; and in that I simply dare not fail. No allowances could be made; there could be no excuse for showing fear in front of them. Regardless of inner turmoil, I simply must appear calm. There seemed only one way to achieve this: to clamp down an iron control on one's natural feelings, and to distract one's mind by positive action of some sort. Not easy; in fact, fearfully difficult, as I already knew. But at least that would be my aim, from tomorrow onwards. That decision eased my mind. I shone a torch on the brickwork of the oven roof a foot above my head, saw how strong it looked, and fell asleep.

Over breakfast the Major told me to work out from the map the details of a shoot at a trench on the Bellevaarde Ridge. We were at the guns for the start of it and then went across the road to our Observation Post in the White Chateau to see the rest. The Chateau, one could see, had been a place of some dignity, standing a hundred yards north of the Menin Road in well laid out grounds. Now there remained but a ruined gateway, jagged tree stumps, and a low mound of brick showing above the white footings of the walls. The Major said it had been Haig's Headquarters at the 1st Battle of Ypres in 1915, but 'red-tabs'* are not seen there nowadays. We entered a door into a low room from which, through a wide concrete slot, several gunner officers were gazing out through binoculars.

From this Observation Post eastwards the ground slopes gradually down to the shallow valley of the Bellevaardebeek, beyond which rises the bare brown outline of the Bellevaarde Ridge. On the map our Front line trench, there known as Junction Trench and its offshoots, was marked in blue, about halfway up the ridge. Just beyond was marked in red the detail of all the German Trenches, plotted by air photography. As these were all in square I on the map, all bore names beginning with that letter – Identity Trench, Idiot Trench, Idea Trench; Identity Support, Idiot Avenue, Iguana Support, Idle Sap, Ignis Trench and so on. We were firing along Identity Lane at a range of only 2,350 yards, or a mile and a third, and soon we could see through glasses the spurts of our percussion H.E.† shells bursting across the ridge.

After our miserable three rounds at Larkhill, it was wonderful to see the real thing at last; to be able to phone through corrections to the guns, and see the shell-bursts conform. For the first time I felt I was at last doing the job for which I was intended. Wagon-line stuff is obviously essential, but to be here at the Gun Position and the O.P. is the real thing. We look the Boche in the face here. He looks at us too. Binoculars are no doubt watching us from the crown of the Bellevaarde Ridge, and also from the line of German Observation Balloons that are anchored in the sky

* Staff officers.
† High-explosive.

in a great arc to the north and south as far as the eye can see. These eyes bode ill for us. Why can't our fighters shoot them down, as the Hun Airman shoot ours down? We cannot see what they are doing, and they must see everything we are doing. I don't like it.

The Major tells me that the new German gas is worse than chlorine, as it raises blisters. Anything such as cloth or sandbags that has been splashed with the liquid or heavily affected by strong gas can blister your flesh if you touch it. They are calling it mustard gas or onion gas, because of its smell. It is heavy and in calm weather hangs around for hours. So rain and a west wind will be helpful to us; but there's no sign of either at present.

Yesterday afternoon three Boche planes suddenly came out of a cloud and went for our sausage balloons, four of whose observers baled out by parachute. Suddenly some of our fighters swooped from the clouds, and in the ensuing dog-fight two Boche planes were shot down in flames, amid loud cheers from the troops watching in the wagon-lines. The third Boche dived right down and machine-gunned the crew of the lorry to which one balloon was anchored, and also sprayed the surrounding horse-lines. Then three of our fighters got on his tail, one above and one on each side. The whole lot roared at full speed over a hedge just near us; and the Boche, having evidently surrendered, managed to land in a field less than half a mile away, while our planes soared up and made off leaving him to be dealt with by the troops on the ground.

Another officer and I ran across and found a huge crowd gathering round the machine. We got close enough to see the airman as he climbed out of the cockpit, taking his helmet off. He was fair-haired and not more than nineteen or twenty. If we could have got hold of him, we would have killed him. Everyone was savage at the machine-gunning, we being so helpless in the wagon-lines. However some senior officers got him into a tent, and before we could let it down on them, a staff car drew up and he was bundled into it. There was an attempt to rush the car, but the sight of senior British officers defending it with sticks checked us, and the car got away. So we reluctantly accepted that he was worth more to the High Command alive than dead – and let it go at that.

His plane was a black striped one, which means that he was a flight commander of Richthofen's Scarlet Squadron. To become members of this squadron they have to shoot down at least twelve allied machines. The captured machine was practically undamaged, and so is a useful prize.

CHAPTER SIX

Overture to Passchendaele

July 18th, 1917. A/112 Bde. R.F.A.

Yesterday I went to see a huge model of the Ypres Salient at Linde Goed Cross-Roads. It was about 100 yards square and showed in miniature the whole country for as much as 7 miles beyond the present German Lines. The soft clay lends itself admirably to this sort of modelling, and it had been very well and accurately done, doubtless from air photos. It showed the main strong-points and dug-outs, fortified farms, pill-boxes, and even important craters. Short lectures and explanations were being given by an officer on a raised platform at the side; I had a vague feeling that one ought to pay for the performance. Perhaps we shall, though not in cash. How can they be sure there are no spies in the audience?

A crowd of officers stood silently round it, making notes. It was easy to read their thoughts. One day soon they will cross the Bellevaarde Ridge in a hail of shells, trying to see where they are, and where to lead their men in that wilderness of shell-holes. But even my short experience suggests that by the time we gunners have done our stuff, most of the landmarks represented on this model will have disappeared into thin air.

The model showed our existing front line trenches, and the main Boche trench system. Coloured lines marked the various positions which our advancing infantry are due to reach by a certain time, following close behind our barrage. This worked well at Messines, though the enemy were so shattered by the effect of the mines that their resistance wasn't effective, and our casualties very light. The coming show is on a vastly greater scale, and there will be no mines because of the low-lying ground. I noticed that the crest of the Bellevaarde Ridge, half a mile ahead, is the first objective, the Blue Line. Next comes the Westhoek Ridge, half a mile further on, the Black Line. Beyond those lie the Green Line and the Red Line; and doubtless more colours as required. To let the imagination roam further ahead seems madly optimistic. I prefer more cautiously the words of the hymn–

> Keep thou my feet; I do not ask to see
> The distant scene. One step enough for me!

This bird's-eye view of the salient shows what a tremendous advantage the Boche has over us for observation. Ypres is the centre of a half saucer with Germans sitting on the surrounding hills watching us from North-North-East round to South-South-East. It was even worse before the Messines show knocked away the Southern prop of his position, and Hill 60. When I look at our gun positions in front of the city, it is astonishing that we can exist there at all, with shells coming at us from all angles. I expect Ypres has been a jolly good investment for the Boche, and he would hate to see us give it up. And equally he won't agree too easily to our smoothing out the salient at his expense. He seems to have air superiority and obviously plenty of guns. But the general opinion is that when all our concealed batteries open up, we shall wipe his infantry clean off those brown ridges that lie ahead, and clear the way for our own 'P.B.I.'.*

We hear that the recent German attack on the Yser Canal north of here was an attempt to capture the flood-gates; and by flooding this part of Belgium to neutralise the purpose of our offensive. A good thing it was frustrated.

Meanwhile the building of log-roads and railways is proceeding fast, and some more first-class Divisions are taking over parts of the line. Batteries of heavy guns and howitzers drawn by motor tractors clatter along the roads by night. Huge ammunition Dumps spring up at crossroads, and all available grassland is taken up with tents and horse-lines, just like a vast fair-ground.

At the gun position also things are warming up. We are firing much more this last day or two. So is the Boche. More shells are bursting among our Brigade batteries, and one has to be much on the look-out, and not loiter in the open. The noise of gun-fire is almost continuous except for a lull between 3 and 6 a.m.

We seem to live in two worlds, one the tense world of the battery position, the other the more or less civilised world of the Wagon-Line and Poperinghe. To be crouching under shell-fire, and then two hours later to be sitting in Pop having your hair trimmed, shampooed and sprayed with perfumed hair-lotion is something of a contrast. Once more to see trees with leaves on them, to lunch in a restaurant with a white table-cloth and a waitress; to sit and talk and smoke in the open with other officers, and to let your ears relax; and

* Poor Bloody Infantry, a term of respect used by gunners.

presently to stretch out on a camp-bed under the warm shade of a canvas tent – and just drift off – oh, it's good!

July 19th. A/112 Bde R.F.A.
I think I may be going up to the guns for good tomorrow. Certainly there has been more firing since yesterday, and things seem to be boiling up a bit. Meanwhile I can catch up on some of your letters.

You ask about Army organisation. Well, starting at the bottom (where I am) – there are 6 guns in a battery, each under a sergeant who has 8 gunners and a lance corporal or bombardier. Each sergeant also has 2 limbered ammunition-wagons under him, with a corporal in charge of each. Each wagon and gun is pulled by a 6-horse team, with a driver riding on each near-side horse and controlling the off-side horse as well. When not taking ammunition to the guns these drivers, horses and wagons are stationed in the wagon lines 4 to 6 miles behind the guns (in trench warfare conditions). In open war, they would be conveniently tucked out of sight behind a nearby wood or hedge perhaps, so as to be ready for a quick move.

My section, when I stop being the odd-job boy and get a settled one, will be 2 guns (i.e. ⅓rd of a battery) with 50 or more N.C.O.s, gunners and drivers, and about 50 or 60 horses. Each battery is commanded by a Major, with a captain to help, usually in charge of the wagon-line. So there are 3 subalterns, with perhaps another sub to relieve them at the guns and help the captain at the wagon-lines. As the guns here may be firing anytime during the day or night, they usually work it that 2 only are on duty, while the other 2 are resting, as and when they can. Of the 2 on duty, one sees the guns are being properly laid and fired; and the other is on the end of the telephone issuing instructions, unless it is an automatic shoot, like an attack barrage, where everything has been prepared beforehand.

All this is as it <u>should</u> be! But subalterns also have to go into the trenches as liaison with the infantry, or to the O.P. as F.O.O. (Observation Post as Forward Observing Officer) and they must be taking up ammunition or reconnoitring new gun positions. Also officers may have to be lent to other batteries, or they may get gassed, wounded or killed. They may even go on leave! Certainly they need an occasional day and night of respite from the gun position, to get a bath and a chance of a night's sleep. So you can imagine what an irregular sort of life we lead – all most unsettling!

Life at the wagon-lines, if less hectic, is very busy. Nearly 200 horses in the battery have to be fed and watered twice daily, groomed when possible, and the forage fetched for them from dumps or railhead. Rations for about 180 men have to be fetched and allotted, and the gunners' share taken up to the guns, with mail and stores, and ammunition. Watering is done at special centralised water-points to which it is pumped in pipe-lines, the ditch water being too polluted for use. It takes some time to take the horses to the water-point and back twice daily. The doctors supervise the chlorinating of our own drinking water in the battery water-cart, but some zealous soul always seems to tip in another shovelful for luck and the result, as often as not, tastes awful, for which the M.O.* gets the blame whenever he comes round.

July 23rd. At Gun Position. C/112 Brigade R.F.A.
Yet another change of address! I'm transferred to C Battery, only a short distance behind A Battery's guns. The officers seem very nice; the Major hails from Auld Reekie,† like a breath of home.

There seems to be a general craze for sending gunner

* Medical Officer.
† Edinburgh.

officers to Trench Mortar Batteries, familiarly termed 'The Suicide Club'. Two subalterns were posted only yesterday, hence my transfer. I was told that I was to stay with this battery. It was implied that the Divisional Artillery Commander, Brigadier General Kincaid-Smith knows of me. I've never seen him in my life, so what's going on? Do I see your hand in this?! Do you know him or have you by any chance moved Uncle Fred* to get in touch with him? I'm sure your intentions are of the best, but for goodness' sake (and for my sake too) leave the High Command to get on with the war on their own! Now that I have landed up with what is reputed to be the best divisional artillery on the western front – the 25th – I don't want to get side-tracked into some other unit; and if other people are really looking for an opportunity for suicide, they'll find it just as well around this gun-position as doing a Trench Mortar course at the base.

The coming show will, it is said, be the most hard-fought of the whole war. The Boche has a great artillery concentration here, but we believe we have a greater. Our present job, and that of the heavies, is to knock out his gun positions, and make life in his trench system unendurable for his infantry. Then when Zero hour comes – and no one yet knows when that will be – each battalion will leave its trenches and advance close behind our creeping barrage of bursting shells. This is being organised so that its forward movement will be precise – 25 yards at a time, allowing the necessary time for the infantry to clean up any machine gun-ners etc in each trench, before following the barrage onto the next. You can imagine how accurate our fire must be and how exactly timed. The whole movement should go like

* Uncle Fred was in fact back in England, having commanded a division in the unsuccessful expedition to Salonika, under the French General Surrail.

clockwork, as at Messines. Compare this with the chaos of ancient battles. It makes you smile!

(Later)

I've been across the road to our O.P. strafing the opposition, under instructions from Brigade. Weather hot and fine; and I expect they can see from our air photos what needs doing over there (we certainly can't) and direct our efforts accordingly. It's very convenient having our O.P. so close at hand as the signallers have much less trouble keeping the telephone going, than if the line came from further forward with more chance of being cut by shells.

Also the less walking one does above ground, the better for one's health. The O.P. is on a ridge in front of Ypres, with the guns just behind the crest of the ridge. If one went further forward one would go down into the muddy valley of the Bellevaarde Beek, get close up to the Bellevaarde Ridge and consequently see less beyond it. Our front line faces the Boche front line on the crest of the ridge, so to us there's dead ground beyond for quite a distance.

Our gun position used to be in full view from Hill 60 – less than 2 miles off to the south. But since the Messines Push, Hill 60 is ours, and now the Boche can't see our guns here, except from his distant line of sausage balloons. No doubt his aeroplanes take our photographs; and when it's fine, as today, they seem to hang around rather more than we like.

We have our six guns in pits, carefully camouflaged with branches and netting; and behind the position runs an old trench with some shallow dugouts which we have been strengthening. A little way behind us are the ruins of a huge Belgian school, marked 'L'Ecole' on our maps, now something of a magnet for shells but that's OK with us here! We have registered our guns, and are not unduly busy at the moment, though there's a lot of our heavy stuff going over our heads.

The Officers' quarters, when not on gun duty, are in the basement of a ruined house. I share a cellar with our Captain, a grand chap who is not only highly efficient, but insists on maintaining the luxuries of life, in every way possible. He has a leather dressing-case full of toilet knick-knacks, with silver-backed hairbrushes, and sleeps in gorgeous silk pyjamas at the battery position, a thing we lesser mortals only dare do in the wagon-lines, and then not in silk! I sleep in my trousers and vest, a bit sweaty but available for action in a matter of seconds. But he's got it so organised that his silk pyjamas would be his 'undies' if necessary – and he'd no doubt be at least as quick off the mark as me. His batman worships him, and takes me under his wing too when I am at the guns, which is very good for my comfort and morale.

It's been so baking hot today, that the gunners were firing stripped to the waist. They look fine with their shrapnel helmets on, suntanned bodies and braces looped round their waists. The only trouble is that we are never free from casual shelling by the Boche, so one moves around with one ear cocked and one eye on the nearest shell-hole. At times the shelling is not so casual, in fact horribly purposeful; and then we get the men off the guns into their dugouts, unless there is an urgent SOS to be answered, regardless of risks. We've been lucky so far that way. Things get much less pleasant at night. Shells seem more frightening in the dark. I find myself listening more, and the bursts always seem much closer than they turn out to have been next morning. Now and then someone gets hit by a piece of shell, but we've had no wholesale casualties so far, which is surprising considering how much the Boche are sending over.

Gas is the worst thing, and we are getting it every single night. We've fitted the dugouts with impregnated gas curtains. But the resulting fug is awful. Gas started coming into the officers' mess dugout, owing to people passing in and out – so we've fitted a second gas curtain as an air lock. So the fug is now even more intense! It's a relief to open up when a breeze blows the gas away.

July 24th. C/112 Bde. R.F.A.

This morning I was in trouble with Sgt. Grouch, a boorish man with an 'Old Bill' moustache. Without instructions he had aligned his gun, taking an angle from a tree-stump a mere hundred yards away, and laying off it without making any allowance for displacement. As a result, he was many degrees off his right line. I was annoyed and in an unguarded moment called him a bloody fool in front of his men. He complained to the Major, who saw us together and rightly reprimanded me. I said I was sorry – and will not do it again, if he lays his gun properly. But I still don't like that moustache.

It's sleep I miss more than anything, and they do what they can to give us an odd night, or even a day, at the wagon-line to make up. It was my turn this morning; so accompanied by a batman, I set off to walk back past L'Ecole. Shrapnel on the Menin Road made it wiser to take to the much-shelled open ground south of the road. When we got within a few hundred yards of the ramparts, the Boche from his sausage balloons was giving poor old Ypres a general dusting up. The Menin Gate on our right and the Lille Gate away to our left were obviously impassable. Over them hung a dull red cloud of shell-fumes and brick dust. Odd shells were dropping on the ramparts and into the town, and the ground in front of us was getting regular bursts of shells from light howitzers. It was obvious that we weren't going to have an easy passage, but with the rosy prospects of the wagon-line before us we decided to have a go.

I noticed that about 300 yards south of the Menin Gate,

the moat was crossed by a narrow wooden foot-bridge, too insignificant to invite special attention from the Boche, and beyond was a little sally-port in the face of the ramparts. For this we accordingly made a series of rushes from shell-hole to shell-hole. Wait for a burst, then ten seconds run, and down; rather like American baseball. We reached the bridge, and although several shells raised great spouts of water from the moat, we got safely into the little tunnel that leads through the massive city walls. No amount of shelling (and they've had plenty) would break them down, and it was nice to be in 'out of the rain'.

The back face of the ramparts consists of great stone arches and vaulted rooms, thickly inhabited by officers with red tabs who are less often seen out in front. Our Artillery Brigade H.Q. is somewhere there, but I wasn't paying social calls. A Captain in the Argyle and Sutherland Highlanders was standing in a doorway, having waited half an hour for the shelling to cease before crossing the town. We decided to join forces, and started making our way through the ruins.

As we followed a narrow path along a street blocked with wreckage, suddenly everything was blotted out with a flash and a roar. Finding a second later that I was all in one piece, I looked up just in time to see an ugly black snout, as of some prehistoric monster, appear over a wall on our left. It was a big howitzer, and I hope her load of trouble dropped on some Boche battery out behind the ridges. On the western outskirts of the town we caught a bus – no longer the London red with gaudy advertisements, but a sober grey – that was taking troops down the line; and so got home without further fuss. I am to take up another convoy tonight.

July 25th. C/112 Bde./R.F.A.
Still at the gun position. The pace seems to be quickening. Yesterday heavy shelling – one dug-out hit, two men killed

and several others wounded. I wasn't at the gun position at the time – but saw some very nasty casualties brought in to the Advanced Dressing Station on the Menin Road.

One quickly manages to harden one's heart and clamp down on the emotions. A month ago the sight of a horse with half its face blown off would have upset me – but now one can't afford to think about it. A wound is simply something to be quickly bound up. A smashed body is not a ghastly tragedy to fly from, but the mere shell, no longer human, of someone who has passed beyond the reach of 'five-nines', and has solved the great riddle. Until that moment comes one has somehow just got to get used to living in constant fear, without ever showing it. This is the *real* battle, secret and silent; and it has to be fought at the same time as the louder and more obvious one – sometimes to the point of exhaustion.

I have been thinking over my shell-dodging journey yesterday with a batman to the Ypres sally-port – a humiliating performance; and bad for morale to be dropping into shell-holes too often. It seems one might be almost as likely to walk into a random shell as to avoid it. In future I shall try to ignore them; but instinct is very strong.

After the roasting weather of the past few days, today it is now pouring with rain. It certainly cleans the air and clears the gas fumes, and everything is much fresher; but it makes the going a bit difficult.

I was sent forward this afternoon with a telephonist to have a preliminary scout-round for a suitable battery position near our front line trenches, so that when we move forward we can get some cover behind the Bellevaarde Ridge. Had a talk with a front-line Company Commander. They seem in great spirits; they are the 8th Division, whom we are covering, and not our own 25th Infantry who are in reserve. From the trenches he showed me the ground. There is nothing one can usefully do at this stage except get a general impression of the lie of the land beyond the Bellevaardebeek, which is rapidly becoming a morass with today's rain.

They seem to think the world of us gunners because, as a result of our heavy fire, they are getting no nonsense from the Boche trenches over the way; in fact they think Fritz has had such a belting that he may have drawn back a bit. They seem snug and quiet, if dirty, in their trenches; whereas they pity us for always having to move around in the open where the shells are falling. Actually, I wouldn't be them for anything; so both of us are happy!

When the show starts I won't have much time to write, but I'll try to send you regular field postcards. Meanwhile, remember, no news is good news.

I've just realised it's a year ago tomorrow that I played my last innings at Clifton. Happy days!

July 28th, 1917. C Battery. Wagon-lines

After being on duty at guns much of the night, returned here in the early hours. Now I have got orders that, as one officer has been killed and another wounded in D Battery, I am posted to them for the period of this offensive. They are 4.5 Howitzers, and although I have a fair theoretical knowledge of them, I have had no practical experience at all. It's rather an awkward time to start learning. Now for a few hours sleep before taking up an ammunition convoy to D Battery tonight.

July 29th. D Battery, 112th Brigade R.F.A.

I am writing this in Battalion H.Q. of the West Yorks, a dugout 20 ft. deep in Junction Trench on the Bellevaarde Ridge. As Artillery Liaison Officer, my tour of duty will be for 24 hours, during which time the big attack may start. Then what?! But at present all is quiet here, though the guns are going at it hammer and tongs; so I've got into a corner out of the way, and will write on my knee.

Early this morning I brought up a convoy of ten wagons for D Battery. We had to drive four miles through a concentration of gas shells, with masks on and lethal gas floating all around. The horses had their new masks on too, and looked very odd. It was surprising that they didn't kick up more of a fuss, but they must be used to anything by now.

At noon I got instructions to go to the trenches as Artillery Liaison Officer, representing 8 batteries, covering this Sector of the line. It was pouring with rain, and it has taken me and a telephonist two hours to cover the mile and a half to here. In many places the communication trench is now flooded by the swollen Bellevaardebeek, and we waded shin-deep in liquid mud. The shell-churned ground will slow up the infantry if we go over the top in the morning; but the rate of 30 yards to the minute for the creeping barrage probably allows for that.

On the way here, we passed a stretch where the communication trench has fallen in or been blown away and we were in the open. Just as we entered the trench again my gumboot slipped on the greasy duckboards and I fell flat on my face, bringing my telephonist down with me. At that instant a whizz-bang burst on the parapet. If we hadn't been down – well you can guess the rest. However it was our lucky day. Further on the trench was lost in shell-holes, in and out of which we scrambled and slithered, often up to our knees in slimy clay, and finally had to go as fast as we could across the open. A few bullets cracked by, but we got to Battalion H.Q. safe and sound, covered with mud and quite exhausted.

My signaller is cosily ensconced with the others in an adjoining deep dug-out, where they crouch round a coke brazier sucking their Woodbines and croaking as the fumes catch their breath. No wonder they look pale-faced; the atmosphere would suffocate anyone less used to it. Even this Battalion H.Q. dug-out has a heavy musty smell, but I welcome it if only to have a few hours relief from the incessant row of guns and shells at the battery position. It's also a welcome change to have a shell-proof roof over your head, so that one can relax a little. I have snoozed for a bit, and spent some time reading back numbers of the Bystander. What a joy Bruce Bairnsfather's cartoons are!

As far as possible, I have prepared for tomorrow morning; plenty of revolver ammunition, my iron ration,* and a first-field-dressing. And I have been trying to memorise the appearance of the church towers in the German back areas, as shown on the card that was dished out at the battery: Passchendaele, Broodseinde, Menin, Roulers, Moorslede and Coekelaere. I can't really believe I shall see any of these tomorrow; but perhaps we may be through in a day or two, inquiring when the next train leaves for Berlin!

Tomorrow morning I shall keep by the Adjutant and hope for the best. It is no use praying to be protected from shells or bullets, when we shall all be in the open together. Why should I be spared? One can only pray for a steady nerve to meet whatever comes. This silver identity disc on my wrist was really brought as an ornament; but if it ever serves a more practical purpose, at least I shall be in very good company.

My job tomorrow will be to help those batteries to inflict the greatest possible damage on the Boche, and to protect our advance – and that I shall try to keep in my mind to the exclusion of all else – so help me God.

(Later)
One wire repaired and working. Well done the linesmen! A message came through that we were going to put down a practice barrage on the Boche lines – which news was quickly passed round, and the infantry were told to keep

---

* A sealed tin box, containing in concentrated form the basic food for one man for one day.

their heads down. Now we have really belted the daylights out of them. With a continuous roar shells went screaming over our heads and burst in a flashing smoking line barely 200 yards away. Our fire was so accurate, that many of the chaps were getting up on the fire-step and shouting 'That's the stuff to give the bastards!' and other quips: I was thrilled, and very proud to be a gunner. The Boche lines more or less disappeared some time ago, and I gather that they are thought to be occupying a line of big shell holes out there. But I doubt if there will be many occupants left by now.

[*The Battalion Headquarters of the West Yorks in Junction Trench, where I did this tour of duty, figures in* General Jack's Diary, *edited by John Terraine, pages 234 to 236. On page 236, Col. Jack describes our practice barrage, which he too watched at close quarters. On page 239 he describes how at Zero Hour on the 31st he 'turned towards Ypres where I saw countless tiny gun-flashes. Our barrage had opened; the inferno was deafening'. Among these gun-flashes were those of our battery. It is good to hear from him, after half a century, that our inferno was up to expectations.*]

July 30th. D Battery. Gun Position

The Battery Commander is a grand chap, Major Sumpter. He's asked me to give a hand with checking over the creeping-barrage tables in half an hour's time. At last here is something that I am really efficient at – back to the Shop classroom!

Major Sumpter has also told me that the cavalry are concentrating in the back areas. Cavalry! This must be IT, at last.

CHAPTER SEVEN

Zero Hour and After

The thundering line of battle stands,
And in the air Death moans and sings;
But Day shall clasp him with strong hands,
And Night shall fold him in soft wings.*

*July 31st, 1917, 10 a.m. With D Battery, 112th
Brigade R.F.A.*
We had fired gas shells last night steadily from 11 p.m. to 3
a.m. at the enemy's forward gun positions. For a time he
retaliated, as on so many nights past, but we had to wear
masks which slowed down our rate of fire. But by 3.30 a.m.
silence fell along the front.

Everyone being very weary, the Major issued a tot of
rum all round, and told the men in each pit that the big
moment had come. All watches were synchronised with

* Julian Grenfell, 'Into Battle'.

Brigade H.Q. by telephone, and ammunition was stacked by each gun with fuses set. By 3.45 a.m. all guns were laid, loaded and checked, quietly with torches. Few words were said. No weariness now. As the seconds ticked by, the men sat in their gun-pits listening to a silence they had not heard for many days past. Major Sumpter stood, watch in hand, and I was beside him.

At 3.50 a.m. exactly, he shouted 'All guns, FIRE!', and the silence was shattered as our guns crashed out in unison with many hundreds of others. The roar of the barrage was deafening. We had to communicate by signs. Such flashing fireworks in the dark I have never seen before. It was the greatest thrill of my life, and I wanted to cheer and cheer again. Then I thought of Junction Trench, the Adjutant, the West Yorks, and the gunner Subaltern who relieved me on 29th. God help them all.

After half an hour of it, I and another Subaltern went back to the Officers' Mess dug-out to be on the 'phone, and ready to check any range alterations asked for.

At 6.30 a.m. I went along the path to the battery position to take over at the guns for three hours. The barrage continued steadily. A dull morning, with rain and dew dripping from the bushes beside the path, and the sinister smell of mustard gas everywhere. Suddenly, rounding a corner, I found myself face to face with about 40 worried-looking Boches led by a cocky little Gordon Highlander, his rifle slung across his arm, and no bayonet fixed. The enemy at last!

My first thought was to shoot some of them. After all that's what we are here for. But the Jock caught my eye, and gave me a wink. After all, he was responsible for them. So I stepped aside and watched them slouch dejectedly by in their dirty grey uniforms and jack-boots.

A little further on another batch of about twenty Boches appeared, this time unaccompanied by anyone. I looked round, but there was no one else in sight. Feeling that these meetings were becoming embarrassing and that numerical odds were temptingly in their favour, I pulled out my revolver, pointing towards Ypres, and barked out 'Get on, over there!' Rather to my relief their leader saluted, bowed and replied, 'Yes sair. Dank you, sair!' And with that they hurried along the path, while I turned away to hide my smile. Too late I thought of adding, in true Woolwich style, 'Double, Damn you! Knees up!' But they needed no urging to put as much distance as possible between themselves and the Bellevaarde Ridge.

When I got to the guns the Major and his Sub handed over to me, and went back to the Mess for a wash and breakfast. We fired steadily for about three hours keeping exactly to the barrage tables we had prepared. Not more than seven or eight shells burst really close during that time, and I have now handed over to another Sub, and returned for a meal.

I am shortly to go forward with two signallers, a pack mule, and various instruments to mark out a forward position for the battery, for we may move forward any moment now. I'll see what trophies I can bag on the way. They say we have already taken over 1,000 prisoners on our little bit of front, and they are doing as well up north. The dressing-station near us on the Menin Road is very busy, with ambulances moving forward and also back through Ypres.

Haven't shaved since I don't know when, and I don't know what my beard will be like by the end of the show. But all's going very well. It almost seems to be a walk-over.

31st July, 7 p.m.

About 3 p.m. a heavy downpour of rain started and shows no sign of easing up. The battery has been awaiting orders to move forward all day, but none have yet come. Rain and mist have made visibility bad, and any rocket signals from our front line wouldn't be seen. It is said that our advance for the moment has stopped and the infantry are consolidating their gains. All our wires seem to have been cut, but a number of S.O.S. calls have been passed on to us indirectly. Boche prisoners and our wounded continue to stream back along the Menin Road, but as is usual in a well planned show our casualties are said to be very slight. I expect a fresh attack will be made early tomorrow morning, August 1st, and then the battery will probably advance. I shall be alone on duty with the guns tonight.

Through the door I can see a gunner singing 'A Garden of Eden just made for two, with nothing to mar our joy!' He is barely audible for the screaming swish of shells from the other batteries, and the steady roar of the rain. With men like these can you wonder that we walk over the Boche? The latter by the way are mostly small and puny. I can see six of the little wretches now, waiting outside the Dressing-station among our infantry. It must feel odd for our chaps merely to ignore men who an hour ago were trying to kill them.

1st August, Noon

Before going on duty with the guns last night, I helped to work out revised barrage-lines in readiness for this morning's attack. It was a real shock to discover that our infantry have had to fall back a long way. And now today they are not attacking, but re-grouping; and tomorrow morning we start once more giving them barrage protection for more attacks only a few hundred yards beyond their original front line. There seems to have been a bad hold-up on both sides of the Menin Road, the 8th Div. in Chateau Wood, the 30th in Sanctuary Wood on our right, where many concealed concrete machine-gun posts withstood our bombardment.

Yesterday our barrage, as arranged, advanced to the Black Line (Westhoek Ridge) and beyond, but our infantry did not even take the Blue Line (Bellevaarde Ridge); so they must have lagged more than half a mile behind the barrage and lost all its protection. Their losses must have been very heavy. Last night I had to answer three S.O.S. calls, firing by map reference.

This morning Major Sumpter sent me forward with a signaller to Hell-fire Corner. But we could not even see the Bellevaarde Ridge through the curtains of heavy rain. It has not stopped raining since yesterday afternoon and still there is no sign of a break. The ground is becoming a quagmire and movement very difficult.

What wouldn't I give for some sleep! Our gunners are worn-out, even though we are firing with half crews at the guns and the others in their dug-outs. But gas and noise make sleep impossible for anyone.

1st August, 11 p.m.

Thank God, I got a few hours' fitful sleep this afternoon. Now we have just finished working out fresh barrage-lines for tomorrow morning. Under the table a chap is lying on a stretcher and is in a bad way. He can't stop shaking and twitching all over. His face is a deathly grey and he is staring vacantly. I've offered him some hot soup, but he doesn't seem to understand anything. The Major says he's badly shell-shocked and will be removed any minute now. No time to ask who he is, as the Major is too busy for anything. We've been fairly heavily shelled today, with some casualties in the other batteries, but so far we seem to be O.K. This blasted rain continues without a let-up. The Devil must be a German and has got control of the weather.

August 2nd, 2.30 a.m.

What a time to be writing; still, day and night are little different to us now. Although we are not in a hollow, the gun-pits have a foot of water in them. We have had to haul the guns out with drag-ropes and bring them into action in the open. The dugouts for the relief crews being flooded out, the only remaining place for them is a few corrugated-iron shelters in a hedge close by, which we have strengthened as best we can with sand-bags. We have fired one S.O.S. and have just got warning, obtained from prisoners, that the Hun is to counter-attack at 4.15 a.m., so I am going to have one hour's sleep before we 'stand-to' to give him a warm reception.

(Later)

These shelters had six inches of water in them, so we've floored them with ammunition boxes and huddled in as best we could, five or six to a shelter. They keep the rain off your head, but that's about all. The 'stand-to' came to nothing, so we managed to snuggle up, worn out, and get another hour's rest. I was in luxury with only 3 others in my shelter. Woke about 7 a.m. and on crawling out saw the fresh crater of a Hun field howitzer at one corner of the dug-out. It had blown part of the outside turf off the roof, yet so deeply had we all slept that none of us heard it. Still pouring with rain. At 10 a.m. came orders to disperse some Huns gathering for a counter-attack in Hannebeke Wood – which we did. Shortly afterwards I was relieved by another officer, and went off duty to the mess to try and dry my clothes and get some breakfast. The usual casual shelling, but nothing very near me, though soon afterwards 2 men were killed by a shell on their way back to the gunpits.

August 2nd, 9.30 p.m.

I can hardly write this. At 2.30 p.m., without any warning, our gun position fairly caught it. Almost the first two shells scored direct hits on our frail little sandbag shelters. The shelters were both full of men, and were blown to pieces. For two hours the position was pounded with five-nines, and some heavier stuff. I was with Major Sumpter and Lieut. Nurcombe, resting in our mess, in the basement of a ruined house close by. We twice tried to get to the guns with stretchers, but the Hun had put down a box barrage and it was suicide to move about. We could not see the gun position for the smoke of the shells. For over two hours the whole area was flying and humming with shell-splinters. We waited in agony of mind – but could do nothing – absolutely nothing.

Then suddenly the shelling stopped, and we went out there with stretchers. The place was a shambles, indescribable, a ploughed field of reeking craters with the guns pointing in all directions. A few men crawled from their little shelters, bleeding and staggering about, and were led away. A doctor came running from the dressing-station with an orderly, and worked on the badly wounded. Men from adjoining batteries helped with the stretchers. When everyone alive had been taken away, we collected what fragments remained of the dead in blankets and sandbags – a ghastly harvest – and laid them in a dugout to await burial.

After a count, the reckoning is that of the forty-six of us at the gun-position, only eleven are left, some badly shaken but game to carry on. Twelve were killed, thirteen wounded, ten shell-shocked. By some freak only one gun was smashed by a direct hit, though all were damaged. There are just enough of us left to man these five guns, at two to each gun, for S.O.S. calls.

August 3rd

Been busy moving the guns into some ruins; clearing gun-platforms and knocking out bits of wall for them to fire through. Everything seems unreal; and with lack of sleep, we work in a daze, which helps to shut out yesterday's horror from our minds.

August 4th

Still with D Battery, or what is left of it. As we have not been firing, we have had time for some sleep, and are beginning to feel a little more normal.

The padre has now buried our dead in a deeply-dug common grave, and marked it with a numbered cross for later identification. The senior subaltern is feeling it a lot, as he lost two very fine sergeants, one of whom had recently won the D.C.M. for bravery under shell-fire. I hardly knew any of them personally, having only been two days with D Battery; but have been helping him to write to their homes.

Yesterday we abandoned the wrecked gun-position; got up some gun-teams and moved the damaged guns back into L'Ecole, the large rambling ruin further back. I don't know what sort of a school it was, but it consists of a number of wings, each with about a dozen cells. Each cell has a small high window and a very solid iron-studded door – more like a prison, than a school. But the cells are dry and a great improvement on our recent mud-hovels. Another subaltern and I have constructed four bunks (two frames of two beds), three tables, and a ten ft. bench – from materials taken from the broken roof, so we are really very comfortable. The officers have the end cell, then our batmen and cook, next the sergeants, and the gunners in the other cells. At the moment, they've almost got one room each. But we hope for re-inforcements tomorrow.

Outside the cell doors there is a high corridor with a brick outer wall. This should act as a burster, so that shells should burst in the corridor and not invade the privacy of our bedrooms. Some other ruined rooms are being used as gun-pits, and at least they have good firm platforms. My two guns are in what appears to have been a large sitting-room or hall. The floor is partly tiled, and the walls are painted, like the drop-scene in a theatre, with oak panelling and windows through which you can get a glimpse of ships on the sea; and even chairs, which you can look at but not sit on. We have had to knock down a bit of the outer wall to let the gun muzzles see out properly.

Major Sumpter is a grand chap, quite young, tall, good-looking, and always calm. All down one side he has had a very big wound – a purple scar about two feet long. I've not asked about it; it seems one of those things that should not be noticed. I should think it needs great guts to come back for more after that lot. He has two children, I think, and writes to his wife daily. He must miss his family terribly. But he has a serene quality which gives confidence and strength to all the rest of us.*

We have a new Colonel commanding the Brigade – Col. Sarson, D.S.O. – who seems very human and friendly. Our 25th Divisional Commander is Major General Bainbridge; 2nd Army Corps Commander, Lt. Gen. Jacob; and General Gough commands our 5th Army; though of course we never see them.

Now for some other points in your letters.

An F.O.O., or Forward Observation Officer, usually takes forward one or two linesmen. When shelling is going on they have to mend the line when it gets broken – a rotten job, I think. Insulated wires are stretched along the communication trenches, and are usually labelled at trench corners. A telephonist winding away at his machine must either have a placid temper or go off his rocker. When contact is urgently needed, you often can't get through, and the chap at the other end appears to have fallen asleep or gone on leave! But they all seem to know each other and realise how difficult things may be at the other end.

Rates of fire vary. For an attacking barrage,

---

* Major G. Sumpter, D.S.O., M.C., was killed in action on 20 August 1920.

18-pdrs. can fire up to perhaps ten or twelve rounds a minute and these have to be checked for aim and range. Fuses are set beforehand. 4.5 howitzers are slower, because shell and cartridge case have to go into the breech separately. For strafing communication lines, fire is slower and more erratic, with intervals of no firing – then the whole battery may fire perhaps only 500 shells in a night.

It's gone on raining heavily now for the best part of a week. There seems just no end to it, and conditions in the valley in front beyond Hell-Fire Corner are simply appalling. The Menin Road surface is solid, except for shell holes, but the ground on either side is an oozing swamp. We shall have an awful job to move the guns through it.

August 6th. D Battery Gun position

At last the sun has appeared, and the ground seems to be a little less liquid; so we hope to move forward soon. We are not firing for the time being except for an occasional S.O.S. from the infantry who are said to be 'consolidating', though how they can find anything solid out there beats me. Masses of planks, miles and miles of duckboards, sandbags, shovels, corrugated-iron, etc., are being brought up the Menin Road by night and just dumped at the side. No more filling up forms for what you want, and not getting it. It's 'help yourself' now – the scrounger's paradise, and the stuff goes as fast as it's brought up.

All today this area has been steadily shelled with 4.2, 5.9, and heavier stuff, but our wing of L'Ecole has not been hit. We were gassed all last night, but without effect. For five hours we could hear the hissing thuds outside. I sat up and read *Punch* in my mask, but found it difficult to achieve the concentration required to see the jokes.

August 9th. D/112 Wagon-Lines

Things look better this morning – and I have been lying around thinking.

What a Mad-Hatter's War this is! Like everyone else I see Germany as an evil enemy, who ruthlessly broke her guarantee to Belgium, and loosed war on her unready neighbours to secure the domination of Europe. Against that we are rightly fighting – for our freedom. But all that is background. The sorry fact remains that I do not hate the Germans personally.

I remember in 1914 the rumours of some of our men being found crucified on barn doors. Raemaker's Cartoons have shown ravaged women and children lying dead in revolting heaps, with an ogre-like Kaiser gloating over them. But that is the world of Grimm's Fairy Tales, and one hesitates to believe any of it.

The only action by individual Germans that has roused me to anger was the machine-gunning of our observers as they hung from their parachutes. Yet when we almost got our hands on one of them to kill him, *that* was wrong; and he was snatched away by our own staff officers.

For the past year it is we who have been attacking the Germans, on the Somme, at Arras, and Messines, and now at Ypres. One cannot blame them for defending themselves and shelling us. Actually these shells that dominate our lives seem to me as impersonal as Jove's thunderbolts. And as the Germans are probably having a worse time of it than we are, it is difficult not to have a sneaking sympathy for them, 'The Boche' or, as the men call him, 'Jerry', seems at most a term of amused contempt; though one must admit that his fighting qualities are not to be despised by a long chalk. But as to positively hating, I somehow don't seem able to; which is all wrong. Perhaps I should join the Infantry and creep about no-man's-land with a spiked truncheon. That might sharpen up one's hatred a lot, and make the whole crazy situation rather more logical.

I have got a pair of thigh waders and driver's riding-breeks from the Quartermaster; so may have some chance of keeping dry when we advance into that sea of mud.

Just heard that our attacks have been renewed today around Hooge and that Bloody Ridge. Hope they'll have better news when I get back to L'Ecole tonight.

CHAPTER EIGHT

Hell-Fire Corner

August 12th, 1917. D/112 Battery

At 4 p.m. on 10th, Major Sumpter and I at last went forward to select our next gun position on the Bellevaarde Ridge. I was to spend the night there with a party of 12 men, digging gun-pits and making a track through the maze of shell holes for the guns to come in by. The party set off carrying picks and shovels, sand-bags and survey instruments. In the sky beyond the ridge hung the usual string of observation balloons which the R.F.C. seem unable to shoot down.

Our intention was to walk straight down the Menin Road, to Birr Cross Roads, turn left, and so on to the lower slopes of the Bellevaarde Ridge. Shattered tree stumps along the road offer some chance of concealment on that blasted boulevarde, but for a hundred yards on our side of Hell-Fire Corner even the stumps of the trees have been blown away. Leaving the twelve men to follow us in groups of two or three, a couple of hundred yards behind, the Major and I, with my servant as a runner, set off down the open road. Out on the left, and also on the right near Hooge, we could see a number of our tanks that had got hopelessly stuck in the mud on the morning of the push.

As we reached Hell-Fire Corner, two large crumps burst on Birr Cross Roads, so we turned off left along the railway embankment. [At that a Boche gunner in a balloon chuckled; but we were not to know it.] Feeling rather conspicuous on the top of the embankment we came down along its left side, but presently reached a big gap which we had to cross in the open. At that instant came the rising shriek of a shell. I crouched down into a shell-hole full of water. The other two flattened themselves against the bank- ing, as a shrapnel shell, perfectly timed, burst above us thrashing the ground with bullets. By a miracle only one of them scored a hit, glancing off my servant's helmet, through a roll of blankets on his shoulder, to finish up in a tin of dubbin in his breast pocket.

We were still on the ground, and I was cursing at the icy slime soaking through my breeches, when a second shell burst just short of us. We did not wait for more, but left the embankment and dashed straight for the ridge, plunging and floundering through the water-logged shell-holes.

Apparently this move saved us, as the Boche could only be sure of pitching his shells along the railway line. He sent over another shrapnel and two H.E.s which fell thirty yards away from us – and then gave it up; while we, exhausted and splattered all over with mud, flung ourselves into a dug- out in Beck Trench which runs along the foot of the ridge.

From this shelter we watched the same trick played on a solitary infantryman. The first shrapnel caught him and he had to be carried into one of the little dugouts in the embankment. It was a nasty moment for us, but a neat piece of work by the Boche in the balloon. Our main party wisely waited, and ran the gauntlet a quarter of an hour later without mishap. Perhaps the Boche was busy celebrating.

Major Sumpter approved the place I had in mind for the gun pits, in front of Beck Trench, where we would be above the quagmire of the stream. He then returned to the battery.

How much better it would have been if we could have worked on the Ridge by daylight, but the Boche balloons made that impossible; so I told Sgt. Hampton who was in charge of the digging party to get some tea going. Beck Trench, though now deserted, had in it plenty of firewood, corrugated iron, planks and duckboards, just what we wanted for the gun-pits, and we busied ourselves collecting it in readiness.

At dusk we got to work; I marked out the gun-pits by torchlight and the cold glare of occasional star shells, and soon all were digging. It was an eerie and unpleasant night. It rained at times. Odd shells fell, always seeming nearer in the darkness. Not wanting to stand idly by, and also in order to keep warm, I took a shovel and joined in the digging. But I was clumsy at it and, so far from encouraging the men, I got the impression that they did not consider it right for an officer to work. So I let them get on with it.

About midnight a hell of a row broke out in front with heavy machine-gun fire. Verey lights went up and a stream of our S.O.S. shells flew close over our heads. The men seemed more frightened than I was, being all on their own in the dark, and wondering if the Boche might be coming at them over the ridge. But when I told them that our infantry were out there in front, and that the hissing bullets were passing well over our heads they felt better about it.

Unluckily, just then some random shelling started, and one burst quite close. There were shouts in the dark, and when I got there I found two of our chaps had been hit by shell fragments, one in the shoulder, the other a surface wound in his thigh. Sgt. Hampton tied on field-dressings and, as both could walk, I sent them with a third man to the 1st Aid Post near Birr Cross Roads. A break for tea in Beck Trench reassured the rest – one of whom remarked enviously – 'Both blighties, the lucky sods!'* It was difficult working in the dark with shielded torches, and the pits were far from finished when in the peaceful interlude just before dawn, I withdrew the men. We returned to the battery by the Menin Road, plastered with mud and dog-tired.

It was hardly possible to sleep during the morning because our guns were firing another attack barrage from L'Ecole. They seemed to make far more noise in the building than they did out in the open. I put ear-protectors in my ears and buried my head under a blanket, but it didn't make things much better. But at least one's body got a rest, even if one's brain didn't.

Then about 1.00 p.m. (that was only yesterday now I come to think of it) the Boche started a 'concentration shoot' in the neighbourhood. It lasted 6 hours. The Major reckoned it was between 3,000 and 4,000 shells, mostly 5.9 with some 8 inch; sometimes a number in quick succession, then an interval, then another lot – average about 10 a minute over the period.

Some of the shells came down with a peculiar scream and a thump that made the whole building wobble; they were said to be armour-piercing, or delay action fuses. In our brick cells after a time the merriment became rather forced. Through one's mind the unspoken question ran – 'Am I imagining it, or is that another one on the way? Yes, here it comes. Keep talking at all costs' – Whoop! CRASH! After a while we gave up the pretence, and looking at each other with a wan smile, consented to suspend the conversation as the climax came.

* A 'blighty' was a wound which was not fatal but severe enough to mean evacuation to Britain.

I started reading *Pickwick*; that is, I held the book in my hand, every now and then turning over a page, but the words which I read and re-read meant nothing. If there had been something urgent to do, distraction might have been possible. But there wasn't. Every nerve was tuned in to the terrifying crescendo of each shell – as they came one after another, remorselessly, jolting the brain as with hammer-blows. As the hours went by we wondered how long it could last. The building was hit several times, and the whole place reeked of shell fumes.

At last the inevitable happened. There was a crash that stunned us, the cell door blew in. Choking fumes and brick-dust everywhere. We could hardly breathe or see. We groped out into the corridor where there were muffled cries for help. A shell had come through a gap in the corridor wall and smashed three of the cells to a mass of brick rubble. This we attacked with our hands. Others joined in with picks and shovels. Soon a foot appeared, and one man was hauled out unhurt. And before long we came upon a helmet, which when removed revealed a head yelling vigorously. With difficulty we got him out. He was almost off his head, his eyes bleeding and blinded with grit. I got a basin of water and tried to bathe his eyes, thinking that if he could see he would calm down. But it was no use, he had to be led away to the dressing-station. Everyone worked away at the rubble, coated with plaster and brick-dust. At last we got out two more bodies, crushed and beyond help.

The Major then decided it was time to go below to the vaults. These were already crowded with sheltering infantry. Here we waited mostly in the dark, for the shock of the shells kept putting out our candles. About 7 p.m. the shelling ceased, and we returned to clear up the mess. There were casualties among the other batteries, too.

We were just about all in when, an hour later, orders came through that we were to go down to the wagon-line to be relieved by another battery. 'And about time, too', was the comment all round. I was sent down the same night with two guns, the rest following next day. Got down safely through Ypres, and slept like a corpse till late this morning, 12th. Now I have been transferred back to C Battery who have lost two officers.

Everyone down here is shocked by the wholesale destruction of D Battery. The Sgt. Major of C Battery says that even the destruction of the famous L Battery R.H.A. at Le Cateau in 1914 was not such a slaughter as ours. I seem to have been lucky. Nowadays, however, people speak not of the destruction of guns, but of batteries; not of platoons but of whole battalions being wiped out. The standard is much more severe by which losses are judged. This morning's attack seems to have made no progress.

We hear all four batteries are going right back out of the salient for a week's rest this evening or tomorrow. I won't say no!

19th August. C Battery, 112th Bde. – at Westoutre

We came out of the line in instalments on 12th and 13th to this rest-camp. I have not written a word in the past week. Here there is green grass and trees with leaves on, and birds singing – and I just let go of everything, and slept.

Weather conditions much better and we all feel more cheerful now. Wagons and guns have been cleaned and touched up, harness re-furbished, our clothes de-loused and our self-respect restored with a certain amount of spit-and-polish, and drill.

This is just the place to put us on our feet again as to morale. We live in smart huts, with cut-grass edgings and white-painted kerbs. The horse-lines and wagon-standings are perfect, and there are hot baths, laundries, decent kitchens, and plenty of time to sleep. It's all run by a Camp Commandant – just like Larkhill, but smarter. Plenty of red-tabs about, but I haven't yet seen any of our own higher command even at a distance, except Brig. Gen. Kincaid-Smith, our C.R.A.* whom I once also caught sight of in the ramparts of Ypres. His Staff Captain, Alston, has visited the batteries regularly, keeping us in touch with what is happening. It has always been good to meet him, and to know that someone back there is actually taking an interest in us members of the Hell-Fire Corner Club out in front. Ours is a very exclusive Club, and we don't have many visitors. I am sure that 'the Staff' find they can think much more clearly in those rooms beneath the massive ramparts of Ypres.

In this week of our reprieve, there has been a chance to adjust oneself to the facts of life – and, for that matter, of death. For out there, it is not just the Valley of the Shadow, but the very home of Death itself, where neither trees, nor plants, nor birds, nor even soldiers can hope to keep alive for very long. First one has to endure the lack of sleep owing to the noise of the guns, which have been rarely silent for days on end; and the interruption from gas attack, and the gassy atmosphere that hangs around the gun position. Then there is the inescapable fear of being hit by a shell fragment or a sniper's bullet in the forward area. My ears must have grown longer and more pointed from listening to the approach of five-nines, and for that split second that tells you whether they can be ignored, or whether to drop flat on your face, tensed for the worst.

Then there is the continued effort of masking one's real feelings, partly from pride I suppose, and partly to avoid weakening the resistance of others. With constant practice I am developing a real poker face, I hope. Thus when you hear that someone you know has been killed, you just say 'Bad luck!' with no more concern than you would show for

---

* Commander, Royal Artillery, of the 25th Division.

a batsman who is out for a duck. It seems that here the very highest virtue is to be hard-boiled.

In this strange world, the Psalms can be a very present help in time of trouble; particularly as they were written by a fighter who knew what it was to be scared stiff. It's really amusing to find how literally some of them apply to life in the Ypres Salient in 1917. 'I stick fast in the deep mire where no ground is' (Psalm 69). 'The earth trembled and quaked: the very foundations also of the hills shook' (Psalm 18). 'The clouds poured out water, the air thundered: and thine arrows went abroad.' (Ps. 77). 'Thou shalt not be afraid for any terror by night: nor for the arrow that flieth by day. A thousand shall fall beside thee, and ten thousand at thy right hand, but it shall not come nigh thee' (Ps. 91). Very comforting that one, so long as you are sure you won't be among the unlucky 10,000! But David was obviously whistling to keep his courage up. Well, there are moments when it's something to be able to whistle at all. But this is surely to regard God as your lucky mascot; and that won't do nowadays.

One has to accept that one's own survival cannot be the first consideration. We have got to beat the Boche, whatever the cost. But this suppressing of one's instinct for safety is not easy, particularly at moments when your stomach turns over and won't go back into place; 'our belly cleaveth unto the ground' (Ps. 44) when the 5.9 cometh! All I hope is that, whatever happens, we may still be able to say 'Our heart is not turned back: neither our steps gone out of thy way; No, not when thou hast smitten us into the place of dragons; and covered us with the shadow of death'.

Forgive this outpouring. It's good to get it off one's chest. Like the eels, I expect we'll get used to skinning; and it will be easier now to keep up the pretence that it's all quite good fun out here, with nothing to worry about but the mud.

Left: Huntly Gordon, 'aged four on a cardboard rock!'

Below: Aged sixteen (*far right*) in the Mayor's House Fives Six team.

Right: 'Having a good eye, I was able to put the bat to the ball and make a few runs.' Clifton College Ist XI.

Above: 'Gun drill with 18-pounders was the real thing. We were soon efficient in every position on the gun.' Woolwich officer-cadets training – the author is second from right.

Above: 'At last the great day came . . .' Passing-out parade at Woolwich, June 1917. Huntly Gordon is the second under-officer with sword.

Right: 'Rather self-conscious in the well-fitting uniform of a 2nd Lieutenant of the Royal Field Artillery.' Huntly Gordon aged nineteen.

'We went down past Hell-Fire Corner and turned left to Rifle Farm.'

'We have our six guns in pits, carefully camouflaged with branches and netting.' 93rd Battery, Birr Cross Road, August 1917.

Above: 'The officers' quarters . . . are in the basement of a ruined house.' The little path on the left led to the guns.

Below: 'It's been so baking hot today . . . the gunners were firing stripped to the waist.' An 18-pounder crew at work.

Above: 'We've been busy piling up ammo for another big barrage and attack.'

Below: 'We rounded up all spare gunners and . . . got the gun slowly out on to firm ground.' Photo taken within a mile of A/112 battery's position at Rifle Farm, 1917.

Above: 'What a treat it is to be able to wash in clean water again; not the foul stuff out of shell-holes.' British soldiers, near Blangy.

Below: 'I led my Section at a gallop about a mile and a half to the rendezvous

Above: 'Next morning we came into action near a farm on the lower slopes, about a mile north-west of Meteren.' An 18-pounder gun crew prepare to open fire near Meteren during the fighting for Hazebrouck, 13 April 1918.

Below: 'And in that day's casualty return, one more gunner subaltern was crossed off the active list.' Stretcher party near Bapaume, 1918.

'I was among a batch of wounded being brought back from Boulogne to London.' Wounded British soldiers lifted aboard an ambulance train, near Douillens, 1918.

Above: Recovering from wounds received: the author with his mother, sister and brother Teddy (who was in the Navy).

Right: Huntly Gordon (*on right*) in 1976, with Stanley Jones – 'a young, dark haired Welshman, very neat and a beautiful rider' – who became A/112's Battery Commander, and who saved his life at Meteren.

August 27th, 3 a.m.! A Battery, 112 Bde. R.F.A.

Due to leave the wagon-line in an hour's time for the same old spot, this time with A Battery. Yesterday I met Nigel Jessop here who was my study companion at Clifton. For three weeks he has been in action with the field-guns only half a mile north of us. He also had a very rotten time, being at one period the only officer left in his battery. The lucky devil is now out of action and on his way south to a place we may go to after we have finished here. He has grown bigger and seems to have aged a lot. But it was a joy at last to meet a friend here. We hope to meet again.

Weather once more appalling. It poured all last night and is still hard at it. Just had word I am permanently (?) appointed to take care of the centre section of A Battery. If these instructions are not cancelled, it will be great to have my own men, and not just be a stop-gap, always being moved around. I envy the rank and file their companionship. It's lonely work being an officer.

(Noon) Back in the line again with A Battery this time, with an advance party to dig new gun pits for them – my speciality! This time the position is not to be on the ridge, but on our side of the stream, just in front of the ruins called Rifle Farm. It's been decided after all that the gun-pits I dug for D battery on the ridge a fortnight ago are not to be occupied yet – they think the ones on our side of the stream are lower down and better concealed. They're certainly lower and getting lower every minute. We'll be lucky if the guns don't sink out of sight!

I inspected the new site this morning, but as it was being shelled and the only cover was a trench with three ft. of water in it, decided to defer work till this afternoon. Digging pits under these conditions is a vile job. The ground is indescribable except perhaps by that one rather out-of-place adjective which the men use for everything out here. But further forward it is even worse. After the first attack the ground was covered with bodies; and for several days wounded men were left to linger on, hiding in shell holes, as it was certain death to go round looking for them.

(10 p.m.) We've made a start, and have finished for the day. I am writing in a dugout belonging to a Trench Mortar Officer who invited me to share it, and who, it turns out, spent last summer golfing at Gullane, and knows many of our friends there and at North Berwick. We had a great chat. Must get some sleep now.

August 28th, 4 a.m.
Weather awful. Cold. Sheets of rain. Clothes wet already. Just off to work. Are we downhearted? Very!

August 30th
Must admit to being at rather a low ebb, having had very little sleep for the past three nights. Weather awful, rain and wind; but the low clouds enable us to work in daylight without sausages staring at us, or even recce planes hovering over our heads. These A-battery men are all new to me, but they have worked very well under awful conditions, egged on with encouragement and repeated brews of tea and a dash of rum. We have finished the six gun pits, though they have several inches of water in them, and built up the sides with sandbags to protect the stacked ammunition. We've also got shelters, above ground, of sandbags and elephant-iron that will at least keep out splinters. There's not much more we can do, so I'm shortly taking the men back to the battery behind Hell-Fire Corner. We're all just about played out. The three attacks in the past week don't seem to have gained any ground at all. While I write this we are being casually strafed; but I've lost none of them so far. Must close and go.

August 31st, 6 p.m. A Battery. Wagon-Lines

I and my new batman, Gunner Harris, and working party were sent down here last night for a rest. Had a long, long sleep, and things look a bit more rosy today. Harris must be feeling better, too. He is outside cleaning my boots, and singing

> O – the bells of hell go ting-aling-aling,
> For you, but not for me.
> O Death, where is thy sting-aling-aling?
> Where Grave thy Victoree?

I am getting to like him.

The Captain in charge of A-battery Wagon-Lines, is Captain Stanley Jones – a young dark-haired Welshman, very neat, and a beautiful rider. The Major, Swinton, is at present up at the battery position. I first met him on that night when I brought ammunition up by Shrapnel Corner, and thought I'd lost the column. He's a very popular Battery Commander so I should be all right; if only they'll let me settle down and get to know my own men.

Incidentally two bits of shells hit me yesterday at the gun position, but not hard enough for a 'Blighty' wound. One piece hit my helmet with a clang and knocked it sideways. The other, a very small tired piece, hit me on the bottom as I bent over. I was wearing my trench coat at the time and it tore a hole, but didn't hurt me.

September 2nd. A/112

I took up the ammunition on Friday night. No trouble. Ypres seems quieter these days than it was when we were preparing for the great push.

Yesterday I left two wagons at L'Ecole, and brought my two guns on to the new position to join the rest. We went down past Hell-Fire Corner and turned left to Rifle Farm, all more or less firm going. Then when we left the track the fun began. The ground had been hopelessly ploughed up by horses and guns when A-Battery's guns had crossed it, and B-battery as well, which is in action alongside us. C Battery, on their right had also done their bit with it. The batteries were firing, registering on new targets – and this made our horses very jumpy. We got the first team over the 300-yard obstacle course, by the skin of their teeth – but the second, upset by a near shell-burst, plunged into an awful morass of mud where they got well and truly stuck, horses, gun and all.

We rounded up all spare gunners, and with the lead pair and drag-ropes, together with boards, planks, etc., got the gun slowly out on to firm ground; and then the limber. Then the other horses one by one were dragged out, covered with mud and trembling all over. But we nearly lost the last horse, for its frantic struggles made it sink deeper and deeper, until at one time only its head and rump were visible. It then gave up and would make no further effort to help. I was in two minds whether to shoot it and push it under; but we kept at it, and after nearly an hour's hauling and lashing of the horse, we slowly recovered it, too exhausted to stand.

All this was accompanied by casual shell-fire from the Boche, mostly percussion H.E. which merely splashed the mud up. But an odd burst of shrapnel caught one of my gunners, and he was brought to me with a shrapnel ball in his back. I could feel the lump like a marble beside the spine, and was tempted to try to prise it out, but thought he'd better be got into more skilled hands; so I slapped on a field-dressing over the hole and got him away to the dressing station.

Now at last we are in position; but first we had to floor the pits with sand-bags to raise the guns more or less above water. They are sitting very high up, covered with camouflage netting of a brilliant green that contrasts much too vividly with the unrelieved brown of this sea of mud. Eighteen guns in a row between the railway embankment and the Menin Road! The Boche balloons watch at times – and we feel horribly naked here.

CHAPTER NINE

In Sight of Passchendaele

September 4th, 1917. A/112

We've been busy piling up ammo for another big barrage and attack. I'm writing from the wagon-line, and go up again tomorrow morning early for four days. We work it in reliefs, 3 officers at the guns, and 2 at wagon-line. There is a steady drain of casualties at the guns, as the Boche keeps up a harassing fire, and shells come from widely different directions when least expected. Everyone agrees that for lack of cover from the enemy guns it's the worst spot ever anywhere. But there's nowhere else to go.

What a blessing our mail and parcels are. For each of us a gleam of warmth and sanity in this crazy nightmare world. We share things as much as possible when they are consumable. I don't need the bath, and it would be rather too cumbersome.* And please don't get me a bullet-proof waist-

---

* This was no ordinary bath. It was of iron and was shaped like a large armchair without legs, tastefully painted in light brown, grained

coat. It would be grand if we could all have one, but I couldn't possibly be the only one.

September 10th. A/112 Gun Position

Weather much improved. Our infantry attacked on our right yesterday morning, where they had been so badly held up. We fired the barrage for several hours – apparently a success.

A gas-shell fell about 30 yards from me this morning. Owing to other H.E. shells, I didn't hear or see it, and the gas being invisible I got a good whiff of it before I could get out of the way. It was an awful moment, and the gripping feeling in my chest made me almost cough my heart out. I had to sit down for a while. However it's now getting better by degrees.

Later this morning we got the backwash of yesterday's attack in the form of a prolonged 'strafe' which has worn everybody out. I sat with some others in a surface shelter by the railway embankment. It was just splinter-proof, and the Boche tried to knock us out all morning. Now the ground is all freshly churned up and shell splinters lie around everywhere. Not many casualties, as we had withdrawn the men to the flank, but a number of gunpits were hit, and the ammunition set on fire. In our particular dug out we played vingt-et-un to distract us from the yowling of approaching shells. That helped a lot. Sitting and waiting for the one with your name on it is a demoralising experience. And the strain of sticking this for five hours on end was such that when at last the shelling stopped, many of us just fell asleep as we sat. Thank God it's over now. But urgent messages have

wood. It was an essential feature of our holiday luggage, being crammed with things of awkward shape and last-minute afterthoughts. Finally it was closed with a large metal lid, and secured with ropes. Owing to its weight and shape, two porters were needed to lift it on to the train.

gone back to replace the bright green camouflage netting with brown!

At one time when I was having a look out of our shelter entrance to see how things were going, something like a scarecrow went flying through the air a good twenty or thirty feet up, the arms and legs out-stretched, turning over and over. It turned out to be a gunner in C battery, blown up by a five-nine. I've never seen anyone actually in the air before. Of course, he was dead, but at least in one piece; not that it makes much difference.

Earlier on during the worst of the shelling we saw one of the men dodging about in the open among the gunpits. He seemed to be visiting each pit in turn along the line of the three batteries. We thought he must have gone crazy as the pits were almost hidden in the smoke of bursting shells, and he hadn't a hope of getting away with it. But every now and then, we could see him emerge and dash for the next gunpit. One of the men in our shelter thought he recognised him as the batman of an officer in B battery – and it now appears that he thought his officer was lying injured in one of the pits. Whether that was so I don't know.

(Later)

We were plentifully gassed last night and I'm afraid this evening hardly gives promise of better things, as they are already chucking a few over. However we are said to be moving out of here tomorrow, touch wood, unless anyone changes his mind. I am to go forward to the front line on Westhoek Ridge tomorrow as F.O.O.; not a very attractive trip, but at least I'll see what's doing out there, and it will be a change from looking at the backside of this Bellevaarde Ridge.

I think I'm immune to colds by now, but I do get rotten heart-burn at times, which is probably due to the gas-tainted air, and bad water.

My trench-coat no longer keeps the water out, and I'm

afraid I may have to get an oilskin coat for the winter, though I believe one sweats in them. Must get some sleep before going forward early in the morning.

September 11th, 3 p.m. On the Westhoek Ridge

I am writing this on a lovely summer afternoon, less than 200 yards from the Boche Front Line.

For the past three days and nights the Hun has been absolutely the limit. Last night we were shelled and heavily gassed from 1 a.m. to 4 a.m. In a lull at 6 a.m., I set out with my telephonist for the Westhoek Ridge. Here, at the moment things are quiet, and with another F.O.O. taking turn to keep watch for enemy movement out in front I can bask in the sun and write. All I really need is a sunshade!

We started off up the embankment of the Ypres-Roulers Railway. About a quarter of a mile in front of the battery we came to what had been the Boche Front Line before the push.

What a place! It was quite impossible to trace anything that had been a trench for more than a yard or two. The whole ground was a wilderness of overlapping shell-craters – A/112's shell craters. I viewed them with professional pride, and awe, thankful to have been at the dispatching end.

We ploughed our way slowly along the line of the railway. All that remained of the rails was a number of broken fragments, some of which had been blown fifty yards or so from the track. A little further on we passed a crater big enough to take a good-sized house below ground level – an exploded underground dump perhaps. It was full of water, green from gas and putrefaction. Most of our dead had been buried, but here and there from the churned-up ground there stuck out the arms or legs of submerged bodies. Most uncanny it was, without a sign of life anywhere. Stakes, wire, sandbags, concrete blocks, Boche helmets and boots (quite a number still occupied), discarded rifles and equipment, trench mortars, boxes of bombs – everything one could possibly imagine, all in the most fantastic jumble and confusion, stretching away as far as one could see both to right and to left. Eight of our tanks sat there, hopelessly bogged down, derelict and obviously there for the duration. But we did not linger as random shells were beginning to fall, and the smell was pretty sickening, even now that one is used to it.

So we went on through this 'abomination of desolation' till in about ¾ of a mile we came on to the famous Westhoek Ridge which we have been persistently shelling for weeks past. Here we left the railway line and struck half-right in the direction of the Rectory Observation Post. My map showed the Sexton's House, the Chapel, and the Rectory; but of these there was of course not a sign, and no means of telling where our troops or the enemy were, except that they could not be far away. As we gazed around for some sign of our O.P. a sniper's bullet went smack against a concrete block beside me, and a voice from under my feet shouted 'Get down, you fool!' – which we did like lightning. We had been standing on the O.P. itself.

The owner of the voice turned out to be the F.O.O. for another brigade, and when I had apologised, he pointed out the landmarks: a prominent concrete pill-box, marked Tokio (can't think why), which was our zero-line – others in the foreground, Anzac and Sans Souci; to the left, St. Joseph's Institute, a huge pile of red brick rubble; Zonnebeke Village just behind it; and beyond that again the ruined red roofs of Passchendaele – and finally in the furthest distance a zone of green trees and vegetation. All this can be seen through a slit between sandbags so that no one from in front would guess we were here – I hope!

All was quiet when we reached here, but at 9 a.m. we were strafed for half an hour. I have a nasty feeling that the arrival of an officer with a telephonist may have been noticed by more than that sniper. We had to retire inside the concrete underground blockhouse that adjoins our little sun-trap. It is without exception the most horrible place I have ever been in. It was constructed by the Boche to face the other way, and now the entrance is in front. Steps lead down to a central passage with two rooms on each side, about 10 ft. square. The rooms are more than half full of stagnant water, and we had to crouch down on planks supported at water level on a heap of corpses underneath. The stench really was awful, and we all had to smoke continuously to keep it down. It must have been full of Boches when our chaps lobbed some bombs in a few days ago. Now frequent bubbles break the surface of the oily scum. We were careful not to stir it up. Thank God, we didn't have to be in there for very long or I would have tried my luck in the open. How sweet was the fresh air and sunshine when we came out.

One likes to think of the Rectory as it must once have been, with some old country priest pottering around, waging war on his greenfly, and taking the dead-heads off his late roses. There are still quite a few dead-heads around, but with a different fragrance. In a corner of a trench nearby, swollen German bodies are actually built into the parapet. That seems to me to be going rather far in human degradation.

I am shortly going to take over, and give the other F.O.O. a spell off. I can see a certain number of shells from other batteries bursting out there on the brown ridges, and though we have no order for any special shoot, I think I'll let off a few rounds. It will at least keep the battery awake and show them there's someone up here too. Each Brigade has its own F.O.O. with telephonist and independent lines, in case one is cut – and it's as well to make sure it's ready and working in case of an S.O.S. – so here goes.

(Later)

I've registered the guns on St. Joseph's Institute; and very nice, too. This is the first time since I came out three months ago that I've had a chance to see our shells burst where I want them to – a welcome change from the perpetual blind barrage as per map. I gave the directions to my telephonist, and presently he announced 'No. 1 gun fired, sir; No. 2 gun fired, sir,' and twelve seconds later I saw the two brown spurts where the shells landed, a little short. A correction of range, then 'Two round gun-fire' and presently a lovely rose-red cloud of dust appeared from St. Joseph's Institute, and I knew we were on target.

Now I've sat in this sunny shell-hole trench for half an hour and reckon I know pretty well the whole geography of this brown valley where the Hannebeek Stream runs out from its wood of skeleton trees.

Although the mile or two of ground in front of us must hold tens of thousands of the enemy, there is not a sign of a Boche at present. The whole place looks completely deserted, as if one could climb out of this trench and stroll across the valley towards Passchendaele, flushing nothing more than a brace of partridges on the way. Well, perhaps hardly partridges; vultures more probably. For respectable birds don't come here. It is a breeding ground only for blue-bottles and carrion rats.

(6 p.m.) All quiet till about an hour ago, when suddenly we spotted figures moving among the trees of Hannebeek Wood. It may have been the beginning of a local attack; but anyhow we each got a battery quickly on the job, and shrapnel twinkled and puffed among the tree trunks. The figures melted away – and all has since been quiet; and our infantry seem happy about it.

My relief, an officer from the incoming battery, has arrived, and I've shown him the ropes. A message has come through that I am to return to the battery at 6.30 p.m., and we're leaving the line. This chap says a shoot is due to start then. Wish the hands on my watch would go round quicker! Must close down and get ready to go.

September 12th
(To resume)

Yesterday sharp at 6.30 p.m., my telephonist and I left the O.P., and on the stroke a practice barrage came down on the Hun Front Line. I wish they'd told me to start a quarter of an hour earlier. As it was, we ran just as fast as the twisty path allowed, so as not to be caught by the enemy's counter-barrage. We just escaped it, but had to pass through the outer fringe of shells, which was most unpleasant. However, except for some more whizz-bangs along the railway track we got back without trouble to the battery position. The last of our battery were just leaving and I sent my telephonist with them; and stayed behind to complete the hand-over. A relief battalion of infantry was moving up the track, the men burdened with their usual loads of rations in sandbags, petrol cans of water, and boxes of this and that. Poor devils, I pitied them. Then I too left, walking back up the Menin Road for the last time.

As I passed Hell-Fire Corner, Birr Cross Roads was undergoing its evening 'strafe', and occasional shells were catching up on me along the road, as if reluctant to let me go. One by one I passed the old landmarks; the White Chateau O.P.; the tragic D/battery site; L'Ecole, more battered than ever; even the oven in which I spent my first night up there. Although everything in me was straining to get away, there was yet a strange fascination about these places, that made me almost reluctant to leave them. They say that a murderer is drawn back to the scene of his crime. Perhaps a near-victim would wish to haunt it too! But reason intervened in the shape of a large motor-lorry, leaving the dressing-station en route for our wagon-lines. They made room for me in the cab – and how reassuring it was to feel that powerful engine going at full throttle in the right direction.

We rattled our way down the slope to the Menin Gate,

still flanked with the wreckage of ambulances and wagons, and still with the eternal stench of gas and decay brooding over the sinister neighbourhood; and back past the ruined magnificence of the Cloth Hall. Then suddenly, emerging from the ruins of Ypres, I saw under a lamp 'N.B.R.' in large white letters – on the side of an ancient engine that stood on the newly relaid railway line. It was like a greeting from an old friend, for that 'North British Railway' engine may often enough have taken me up from North Berwick to Edinburgh Waverley – or other parts of Scotland, now so far away. At last we reached the wagon-lines, and with a cheery 'Goodnight, Sir' the lads drove off into the night.

For a while I stood alone in the friendly darkness, breathing in the fresh night air – no taint of gas, no sound of shells. It seemed unbelievable that I had been given another lease of life, when so many others had not. Across the field, lights shone out from the Mess-hut. Occasionally a horse whinnied in the horse-lines; and tomorrow we would be on the road, away from it all. Away from an Inferno hardly less terrible than Dante's own, 'whence issuing we again beheld the stars'. And I too gazed into the inscrutable, yet comforting, peace of the night-sky; and thoughts ran through my mind which I have no words to express.

Harris was waiting for me in the Mess with a cup of cocoa. He fussed over me like a hen with one chick, and pressed me into taking a strong nip of whisky. And saw me into bed, dead-beat.

CHAPTER TEN

Pastorale

*September 12th, 1917. Godevaersevelde, A/112 Bde.
R.F.A.*

Soon after mid-day we pulled out from the wagon-lines,
and marched away westwards. For a time I kept with my
centre section – gun, wagon, wagon; gun, wagon, wagon –
taking a good look at the horses and men under my
command, many of whom are new to me. But as soon as
opportunity offered I rode joyfully forward to report
progress to Major Swinton, and then all the way back to
Captain Jones at the rear, it being the first time I have seen
a whole battery on the march before. We stretched well over
a quarter of a mile, the rear being brought up with G.S.
Wagons, field kitchens, water cart, mess-cart and the rest.
Most of the horses were in good condition with a gloss on
their coats from daily grooming; and a brave show they
made.

By late afternoon we reached Godevaersevelde, a

delightful spot where we are now camped in tents around an old French farmhouse. My charger Molly, and my second mare Kitty are piqueted by my tent. Molly is having a soothing roll on the grass. Here there is nothing to remind us of war, except for the nearby railway where trains continually puff up and down carrying more men and munitions to the line. Our 9 mile march has not only shaken off the dust of the Ypres Salient, but has brought us from Belgium into France. The civilians somehow look different – rather less stolid, perhaps.

September 14th, Godevaersevelde

It is a most curious feeling to be here. One feels the silence so much; yet it takes a positive effort to relax. I cannot yet rid myself of the unconscious habit of listening for approaching shells. Last night I woke up wondering where I was, and why it was so quiet.

Yesterday, with the A section subaltern, John Wilson, I rode across country to Hazebrouck. We had coffee and meringues in a restaurant, and then sat in the square eating liqueur chocolates. Presently the town band entered the band-stand in the square and played a gay selection. (Yes, this is France all right!) We whistled and hummed for sheer joy, as if we had just been released from prison.

What a treat it is to be able to wash in clean water again; not the foul stuff out of shell-holes, which had to be boiled, and even then looked and smelt thoroughly contaminated.

These two days have been spent cleaning guns, wagons, horses, harness, uniforms, everything; and having a few parades just to remind us that we are now the Royal Artillery once more, not mud-larks as for many weeks past.

Have just had the great news that I am to get 10 days' leave before the end of this month. Have ordered a new pair of riding-breeches from my tailor – the very best.

Answering your questions, each of us carries a first-field-dressing, which includes an iodine ampoule, which one breaks and dabs on the wound. We are encouraged to do this with even minor cuts and scratches, because the contaminated ground is so rich in germs. It's not possible to know when you will be in action or when at the wagon-line. You just go where you're sent. I once had a whole week at the wagon-line, but also had four weeks more or less continuously in action, before and during the push. The infantry are in the front line for only one or two days before they are relieved – but then none can spend longer than that in the cramped conditions of the trenches.

The guns in the photo you sent are eight-inch guns and have a range of about fifteen miles. This enables them to be sited a long way back from the front line, where they are themselves out of range of the Boche guns, so they need no gun-pits and very little concealment, and as the crews are not under fire they don't need to wear tin-hats or gas-masks. My guns are 18-pdrs, and are often within 1,200 yards of the front line, never more than 4,000 yards. So we are sometimes within rifle and machine-gun range, not to mention every type of Boche shells, including gas-shells. Hence our need for gun-pits and concealment. We are the smallest of artillery, but the most advanced and the most quick-firing.

(Later)
Today John Wilson and I rode into Bailleul,* a quaint and beautiful old town. We had a bath and a haircut, and then went to the Officers' Club for lunch. The main dining-room was full, so we entered a smaller room, and were at once dazzled by a blaze of red-tabs and medal ribbons. But seeing a small side-table empty we sat hurriedly down, and had

---

* On the way we passed through Meteren, a village I would return to in due course.

another look. The important officers were so deeply entrenched behind a parapet of flowers, fruit and wine-bottles that it was not easy at first to see them. But presently by peeping over our menu-cards we saw the white moustache and rosy apple-cheeks of General Plumer, our Army Commander; the tired blood-hound features of Sir Edward Carson; and the inscrutable parchment of Lord Milner's face.* Soon a waiter suggested in a hoarse whisper that this was a private lunch and we should leave. To which, in equally hoarse and even thirstier whispers, we replied that there was no room elsewhere; that we wanted the best of everything, and had evidently come to the right place for it; that we would only leave if the General ordered us to; and would he please bring the wine-list without delay.

After a short while the party broke up, and a little insistence got us a share of the cake, peaches and grapes with which their table was richly furnished. We felt that, after Ypres, we were jolly well entitled to it. But we also lost a great opportunity for, five minutes after they had gone, a distraught staff-captain appeared in the doorway, scanned the table anxiously, dashed forward and retrieved from behind a large vase of flowers a bottle of whisky, which he bore triumphantly from the room. This prompted us to give the table a further look-over; result – a couple of large cigars, which we felt sure that General Plumer would have wished us to enjoy.

* Lord Milner and Sir Edward Carson were both members of Lloyd George's inner War Cabinet. The purpose of their visit, as is now known, was to discover what justification there might be for Haig's dogged persistence with the Passchendaele offensive in spite of the terrible losses being incurred. It is an arresting thought that, if only this lunchtime discussion had been held in the more realistic atmos-phere of the Westhoek Ridge, with the Commander-in-Chief in attendance, that ruinous offensive would most probably have been called off long before our casualties reached the appalling total of 400,000.

Sept 18th

Bad news! Our leave has been stopped for some reason, so it will be 3 weeks before I go at the earliest. I hear Horatio Bottomley has been nosing around here, doing the back area trenches with a tin-hat on; so you may perhaps read in next week's *John Bull* 'startling revelations of gross incompetence in high quarters' etc! (Please excuse this mess, but the sheet blew away and I just caught it with my boot!)

Two days ago we marched twenty miles south west, through Hazebrouck, to a little hamlet called Wittes, by the side of a canal. Here we watered and fed the horses, parked the wagons, and had tea at the farmhouse, where I am now billeted. I have a little bedroom with lace curtains at the window and an enormous feather-bed, into which I sink so far that it almost closes over me – a bit of a change from the stretcher I usually lay on at Ypres.

After tea, Wilson and I lit our pipes and, feeling at peace with all the world, strolled down to the canal. It was a lovely scene. At our feet the glassy surface of the canal, reflecting the vivid blue of a cloudless sky; a little row of white-walled red-roofed cottages by the waterside; on a grassy rise the old grey windmill, and close beside it the miller's house with the thatched roof. Gliding slowly towards us was an old black barge pulled by two women in blue dresses and wooden clogs. A man reclined at the tiller smoking lazily. As he came abreast of us, I asked him in my best French, which rather to my surprise he seemed to understand, why he sat there and let the women do the work. The old rascal replied that he was the only one skilled enough to steer the vessel!

Unfortunately, we only spent one day in this beautiful spot and have now moved twelve miles south to Amettes, which lies in a wooded valley, a few miles west of Lillers.

September 26th. A/112 R.F.A. at Amettes

For the past eight days we have been officially 'resting', which means a non-stop succession of parades, inspections, drills, tactical schemes, and sports, with three practice shoots on a nearby range. It will be a relief to go into action again if only for a little leisure! Leave has been cancelled, but no reason given.

I hear that the gunner-batman who searched the gun-pits under heavy fire at Rifle Farm was recommended for a V.C. But he was apparently under a deferred sentence of imprisonment for indefinitely overstaying his leave. So his bravery (desperate perhaps) was rewarded by the cancellation of his sentence, and a D.C.M.

At last I am getting to know my chaps, and what they can do. My two sergeants are really fine men; Durney, a Dorset man, rather silent but utterly reliable, with penetrating blue eyes and a heart-warming smile; and Lindfield, a farmer in civil life, tall and fatherly, a little slower, but very sure.

Battery Sergeant Major Howes is a real character. A true Cockney, ex Welter-weight Champion of the Indian Army; a boxer's broken nose, a jutting chin; and a way of standing poised and leaning slightly forward, as if about to jab his left into his opponent's face. There is hidden menace in his husky voice, and the men have a healthy respect for him, so he really gets them moving. Me he tolerates, showing little deference to an inexperienced officer less than half his age, which is reasonable enough. Quick-witted and cheerful, utterly unconquerable. In fact the ideal B.S.M.

We seem equally lucky in our Battery Quartermaster-Sergeant. Not at all a military figure is Q.M.S. Thurlow, but his slogan is – 'If you want it, I'll get it.' And he does better than that, usually guessing what will be wanted before it's asked for. Has lots of initiative and a firm belief that the end justifies the means. As 'the end' is always in the interests of A/112, we do very well as a result of his efforts.

Then the oddest character of them all, Sergeant-Farrier Dance – a Falstaffian figure, with a loud voice, fearful invective, and a ready laugh. Regards Army methods as a joke, and is quite unmilitary; but an absolute wizard in anything to do with horses or mules. He is a Scot and hails from Strathearn, to our mutual pleasure. He told me that he had got out here by giving his age as forty-six (really sixty-four!) and volunteering for *unpaid* service. That may be just his yarn, but he is a real treasure, and I have already learned a lot from him. He rarely wears a tunic – except at parades, when he hovers in the background with his tunic half-buttoned and his cap on the back of his head. Officers who know him look the other way. He would be unreplaceable.

I was taking 'stables' the other day, and paused opposite a black horse called 'Snowflake'. It had been groomed and was standing well back from the tethering rope to which its head-rope was attached. Its ears were laid back, the whites of its eyes were showing and it had a thoroughly evil look about it. I was just thinking 'You're a nasty looking brute', and turned my head for a moment when BANG! Something like a battering-ram struck me in the chest, and I was half lifted off my feet. I gave him a full right hook, and he let go and retired behind the rope. A corporal ran up to ask if I was all right. Feeling as if the front of my chest had been torn off, I assured him I was.

When he had gone I slipped my hand into my tunic and was relieved to find no blood. My Sam Browne belt and tunic had just been enough to prevent his teeth meeting in my flesh, which is now black and blue. Either I must have a very expressive face or that horse is a thought-reader. They say his driver is the only man who can handle him. Perhaps he was a lion-tamer in civil life.

The other sections have got remount mules for their gun-teams, some of them pretty sprightly. Two especially have a nasty glint in their eyes, and it is noticeable that the horses on the line keep well away from them. The other day at feeding time a driver approached these two with their nose-bags, but quickly had to retire in a flurry of hoofs. Then his sergeant, with a cutting remark as to the driver's lack of skill in handling mules, took over the nose-bags and advanced warily. At four yard's range, the mules' ears went back and they cleared for action; at two yards there was a flash of hoofs, and the sergeant escaped a 'Blighty' or worse by inches. As he emptied their feeds on the ground in front of the rope, his remark was short and to the point; 'I always thought my missus 'ad a temper; but she's suckin' 'oney to these bastards!'

But for all that, one can't help admiring these mules – and in a tight spot I'd sooner have a team of them than of horses. Mules are usually much steadier under shell-fire; they are hardier and can do better on short rations; only one mustn't argue with them or try to pull them about; just walk firmly ahead, head rope in hand, and they usually follow quietly. I admit they haven't the fine spirited appearance of a good horse, but out here it's more important to do the job well than to look impressive, which probably applies to us too! So if some of my drivers look like muleteers or gauchos or whatever it is, I don't mind so long as they can get the mules to do what is asked of them.

There is a lot in choosing horse-teams – almost as much as in selecting a cricket team. The gun team, of course, must be the best of all, both drivers and horses, for they must be able to take the guns over the worst possible ground where the other teams cannot go. Pack horses can always bring up the ammunition if the ground is too bad for limbered wagons. Of the gun teams, the lead driver and horses must be outstanding, a lion-hearted trio, ready to tackle anything and quick to pick the best way through bad ground without any hesitation. Next in importance are the wheel horses, which must have the power and guts to keep pulling until they drop. Slightly less important are the centre pair, following where they are led and taking their full share of the load. And as usual, it's the team spirit that counts.

September 29th at Amettes

At the recent Divisional Sports and Horse show, my section was selected to represent A/112 Battery in the Alarm Race. In this, the whole section took part, consisting of two guns, four limbered wagons, with the gunners and drivers and thirty-six horses. At the start we all had to pretend to be asleep; the horses picketed to the wagon-wheels, all the harness in heaps on the ground, the men lying down with their coats off. At a signal from a trumpeter, everyone jumped up, dressed, harnessed his two horses, hooked in the teams to the guns and wagons, mounted and formed up. I had the relatively easy job of catching and saddling up my charger, and taking command. We then advanced at full gallop for 100 yards. 'Halt, action front!' – teams away, guns into action, laid on target, and both fired one round of blank. All this we managed to do in 3 minutes 40 seconds, which was not so dusty seeing we had never done it before. We came third, out of the eight batteries competing.

Sir Douglas Haig was there for a short time to decorate various people. Major General Bainbridge, our Divisional Commander, presented the prizes.

This had been our last fling before going back into the line tomorrow. It's been good to be with the other batteries, and we are in good fettle once more; though I wish I could stop having such vivid dreams.

There is only one thing I regret – the lack of regimental tradition. We are a very efficient bunch of amateurs, brought together for this war only. The infantry regiments are much to be envied for their regimental traditions and customs. It would be nice to feel that one's forebears had fought in the regiment before, or that we all came from the same part of the country, and at least had a geographical background in common. It would bind us together more; and that, to me at least, would mean much.

Tomorrow night, 30th September, we are going into action again just south of here – a coal-mining centre resembling part of a telescope.* All I know is that it is said to be extremely gaseous; but our battery position is bound to be better than at our last place (how could it be worse?). Though quiet of late, I expect we shall wake it up, and it will be surprising if we don't take the place. Though why we should want to, we just don't know. Perhaps the coal will come in handy for the winter!

October 3rd, 1917. A Battery, 112th Brigade R.F.A. At Lens

On 30th Sept. we left our happy valley, marched through the ruins of Bully-Grenay, and have taken over a battery position in the western suburbs of Lens. It is a comfortable position in every way, with gun-pits cleverly concealed in long coarse grass. We live in old Hun dug-outs, twenty feet below ground. I'm amazed at the amount of work and concrete the Boche use for their protection. We welcome such quarters where we find them, but would never go to all the trouble of building them for ourselves. I believe we would regard it as a sign of 'wind-up'!

When I came up for two days liaison duty with the infantry I found them in very poor quarters. My signaller joined the others in their telephone dugout, where all crouched round a charcoal brazier, warm though semi-asphyxiated. I reported at Battalion H.Q. in a cellar.

When we sat along the table for supper, the Colonel put me on his right, and went out of his way to be nice to me.

* Lens.

It was obvious that some of the other officers disliked him, which was why he bothered to get me on his side. He drank a lot, and didn't leave this cellar during the two nights and days that I was with them. Perhaps his nerve was going.

On the second night, at midnight, the enemy suddenly put down a heavy trench mortar and field-gun barrage on us, which we took to be the prelude to a raid. Furious machine gun fire broke out, with a pandemonium of noise. My signaller almost at once reported our line to the battery cut; and when the Colonel asked for 'S.O.S.' fire, we sent up Verey Lights and my signaller did his best to repeat the message by flashing his signalling lamp from the upper part of a ruined building.

In no time at all shells were screaming over our heads to burst in No-Man's-Land, and the darkness was brilliantly lit by the flashes and magnesium flares. Soon a runner looked in to report that the enemy had attacked, and been driven back by machine-gun fire; but that there had been many casualties from mortar-fire in our front line.

Things presently quietened down, and as the Colonel showed no sign of leaving H.Q., the Major asked me to come round with him. He led the way first to the front line trench, where they had had a very rough time. The men seemed very glad to see him. They were amazingly cheerful after what they had just been through. Whole sections of the trench had been blown in, and they were still digging for bodies. It was a terribly slow and painful business getting stretchers with badly wounded men down the communication trenches. Much work had to be done hurriedly in the dark in trying to restore the front line trench. The final toll was five dead and twenty-six seriously wounded.

When we got back to H.Q., I happened to be the last to enter the dug-out – a process which had to be carried out backwards, owing to the way in which the stairs were built – and I had just put my head out for a last look round, when a high-velocity shell whizzed past about five feet away and burst fifteen yards down the trench. It gave me such a start that I did a high-velocity descent down the dug-out stairs with the loss of two buttons off my tunic.

The Major was quite pleased that this Boche raid has been a failure from the point of view of getting prisoners and identifying the units holding our part of the line. The Boche can't know how many casualties he has inflicted, any more than we know how many Boches have been killed by machine-gun fire, and our barrage. It must have been a lot, as they didn't reach our trenches.

This trench raiding is a strange business. I think the infantry hate it. The Major does not believe that even if they succeed in identifying the unit opposite it makes any differ-ence to our plans. There are easier and better ways of spotting a coming offensive. Probably someone high-up and rather out of touch thinks that trench raids will keep our infantry on their toes, and 'cultivate the aggressive spirit', etc. Out in front, they just don't believe that the results justify their casualties. Yet they must obey orders – P.B.I.!

Now we are out of the line once more, the Lens attack having been cancelled for some reason. They can keep the place, slag heaps and all, as far as I am concerned.

October 19th, 1917

We've marched through Bethune and are camped just north of the Bethune–La Bassée canal, an idyllic spot. What is even more important is that leave has started again, and I am third on the list, so I may get away in two or three weeks' time (the Boches and our own High Command permitting).

This is an unbelievingly cushy spot, opposite Givenchy, where the front line has remained unchanged for two and a half years. It's like a dream, after Ypres, and we wonder when we arc going to wake up.

The Officers' Mess at the gun position is in an untouched house a bare 2 miles from no-man's-land. At that range in the Ypres Salient there was nothing but destruction and desolation. But here beside us lives a French woman with three little daughters. The men are billeted in an adjoining farm, where each man sleeps on a wooden-framed wire-netting bunk. The ground in front of the guns is mostly turnip-field, where white-haired old men in blue smocks and wooden clogs work away, guiding the plough round the occasional overgrown shell-hole. There are even seed cabbages in no-man's-land. They are not actually cultivated there, but I'm sure the infantry don't let them go to waste.

And to cap it all, I now have an independent command of my own, a detached section of two guns, sited two miles north of the battery. These are laid on S.O.S. lines enfilading no-man's-land at Givenchy, because it is too narrow (only 30 yards between the front line trenches) to allow S.O.S. fire from behind. We rarely fire; but spend our time improving the gun-pits and the men's billets. We have already made good fireplaces and installed a zinc bath.

On the plaster walls of these rooms there are pencil drawings of the crests of famous Highland regiments, done by the Jocks on the eve of the battle of Festubert. 'Remember us,' they seem to say. That was two long years ago, at the time of the Asquith shell scandal. Poor devils, they had to attack without a covering barrage, and were mowed down by the German machine guns.

There are masses of jolly good apples in the orchard where we are concealed. Six of my thinner horses are grazing in a paddock in front of the guns! These have to be rounded up before we open fire in the daytime: but then there is little risk of an S.O.S. being needed at short notice.

There are only fourteen men in this little command, but we are all enjoying ourselves and look forward to spending the winter here. Perhaps we deserve it after those three months at Ypres. It has now been officially stated that, there, we were directly opposite the greatest concentration of artillery the Hun has ever assembled. At the risk of seeming ungrateful, I must admit that was an honour we could have done without, not being exactly greedy for glory.

October 24th. A/112 Bde. R.F.A.

Back at the Wagon Line. Been asked to teach some of my new men riding. I managed to put up a passable imitation of a Woolwich Riding Instructor – 'badinage' and all – which made them sit up a bit. Some of them are not very good riders, especially on mules.

In the past month we have lost three subalterns (one sniped, one gassed, one chronic rheumatism) and the Captain is on leave; so I have been acting second in command of the battery, and for the last three days had charge of the wagon line, about 150 men and 150 horses. Plenty to do.

October 28th

Col. Sarson has just told me to go on leave tomorrow at noon. It seems too good to be true.

[*That ten days' leave went so fast that I recall it only as a series of snapshots. The white cliffs; the people waving as we drew alongside the quay; welcoming smiles from total strangers; the cosy familiarity of the little fields and gardens from which people waved us home. These went to the heart, and it took all my poker-faced training to keep outwardly unmoved.*

From London I took the Bristol train. Back at Clifton I found security, sanity and the welcome of friends. In the evening, among a group of Old Cliftonians round our housemaster's fireside, I heard with delight the gossip of the school; and, when the fire had sunk low and the beer was exhausted, I slept peacefully in the house I knew so well.

Thus Clifton laid her healing hands on me; and the grim spectre of Ypres faded into the background like an evil dream.

After the next night in the train, the following morning saw me nearing my Edinburgh home in an ancient growler, whose leather cushions smelt as if the horse itself was accustomed to sleep on them. Home was – well, home.

And after that came a seemingly endless succession of friends and relations, who all inanely asked 'How are you getting on out there?' to which I invariably replied (with my thoughts firmly on that Givenchy apple orchard), 'Fine, thanks, just fine.' What else could one say? How could they begin to understand? We were now simply in different worlds.

All too soon came the farewells; the reluctant return to London; a seat at 'The Bing Boys'; and the walk back through the shadows of Leicester Square past a long line of clucking old hens, whose furtive endearments only caused me to quicken my step. There was by now a girl's photograph in my breast pocket.]

November 14th. A/112 Bde. R.F.A. Festubert

The guns up north are once more going hell for leather, just like continuous thunder, for two days past. Canadians having at last taken Passchendaele, what happens next? Everyone has long ago given up any idea of a break-through.

Nothing here has changed since I went on leave. Along the cool sequestered vale of life, we keep the noiseless tenor of our way. Both sides seem content to ignore each other in this sector. In fact it is so peaceful that the other afternoon, having to go to Battalion H.Q. in the trenches and not wanting to push my way up a long communication trench, my groom and I rode together from Windy Corner straight along the disused road towards Givenchy Church. H.Q. is underground in the basement of a ruined house, and though it is barely 500 yards from the Boche front line, not a bullet or shell came near us. But the infantry were rather surprised as they gazed up at us from below ground level. It was a funny feeling to be riding over trenches and through gaps in belts of barbed wire, knowing that hundreds of men, friend and foe, are there; yet with no sign of anything but a thin wisp of smoke rising from the Hun lines where someone is presumably frying sausages for tea. I dismounted and climbed down into the trench, and my groom made off down the road with both horses. But I've been asked by the Company Commander not to do it again.

November 23rd. Near Givenchy

At last there has been a successful break-through south of here (Cambrai). The procedure was apparently the very opposite of Ypres, i.e. no artillery preparation at all! Our tanks just came up and drove through the wire and the infantry followed them, with a success that surprised everyone. We heard we were to move there quickly; then that was countermanded. The Boche was able to organise a counter-attack, and it seems that the whole thing will probably fizzle out. But this new fashion in attack is infinitely better than the old one – provided always that the enemy is taken by surprise.

Life is so pleasant here that I'm sure it is too good to last. Bethune is close by, and hardly damaged at all – a nice little town, where the men can go shopping and sample the estaminets and anything else that's available. There is a good Army canteen, and an absolutely first-rate pierrot troupe; though admittedly we are easily pleased. They didn't have pierrot shows at Ypres; and if they had I doubt if they would have got many laughs. Our emotions were frozen; but here we can relax, and the laughter comes easily.

There are no women in the troupe, but two men who make up so well that you would hardly know the difference. They sing plenty of sentimental songs. My favourite – to a lovely tune – is

> From Somewhere in France to somewhere in Somerset,
> When shadows are falling, my heart's to you calling.
> May angels all bright and fair, watch over us both with care
> So that some day I'll come to somewhere in Somerset.

I hope I've got it right, though I'm not sure about the 'us both with care' bit! Anyway we all sit there in rows, singing our hearts out, as far as the lumps in our throats will allow.

Another good song is at first sight thoroughly defeatist. It should be sung in the manner that musicians might call 'maestoso' – very moist – the time being a suitably melancholy waltz rhythm:

> I want to go home.
> I want to go home
> Shells and 'Jack Johnsons' around me roar.
> I don't want to go to the war any more.
> Take me over the sea,
> Where the Allemand can't get at me.
> Oh, my! I don't want to die.
> I want to get home.

I wish some Boche could hear us, I'm sure he would report a complete breakdown of British morale. I've no idea about the psychology of it; all I know is that it relieves the feelings. Perhaps it's the way the crazy British shrive themselves before battle, as the Germans may yet find to their cost.

November 25th. A/112 Bde R.F.A.
Back at my detached section again. We had left a sergeant to

run it, but things had got slack, dirty billets, etc, so I have come over for a week to smarten them up a bit. I have been on the strafe today and I expect tomorrow everything will be ship-shape again, and I'll have nothing else to do for the rest of the week. My servant, Harris, is a great asset on these occasions. He's also a very good conjuror and does tricks with cards and coins under my very nose, which leave me baffled and admiring. He is a quiet, stolid type, very reliable, and I am really lucky to have him.

(Later)

This evening we have just had the most exciting S.O.S. – I don't know what this peaceful place is coming to! Apparently, the Boche tried to dispute the possession of a shell-crater in no-man's-land with one of our outposts. Anyhow we had an S.O.S. phone call and within half a minute my two guns were firing flat out. One gun detachment was rather short-handed, so I joined them as one of the crew. We worked up to a speed of nearly a dozen rounds a minute, about the fastest possible. The gunners have to seize a round, set the fuse, load, close the breech, lay the gun, fire it, open the breech extracting the brass cartridge case – all that in 5 seconds; soon there was quite a pile of cartridge cases round the gun. Then suddenly the camouflage netting round the mouth of our covered gun-pit caught fire from the blast.

This camouflage is wire netting covered with green tabs of sacking, soaked in cresol, so you can imagine how it blazed! A brief pause, while two gunners tore away the blazing stuff, and we resumed firing. Then after four more rounds the whole camouflage over the roof of the gun-pit was ablaze, with some risk to our ammunition. I jumped up on the roof and threw the netting on to the ground, where the crew tried to stamp it out. This was no good, so we dragged it still blazing to a shell-hole full of water and jumped on it till it was out, and we were soaked. At this point the Boche started trying to neutralise us with gas-shells. This was the last straw! We shoved on our gas masks and resumed firing, though at a much slower rate; and soon after, the S.O.S. ended – and the gas-shelling ceased.

A nice mess we were in! Our fingers burnt, our faces blackened and our eyes smarting with the smoke of the burning camouflage, and our legs soaked from dancing on it in the shell-hole. And I for one am still deafened with firing in an enclosed gun-pit, where there is twice as much noise as in the open. The gas has cleared off, though the place still stinks of it; but we got through with no casualties and everybody very happy. We hope the infantry in Givenchy trench are as well off. A bit of excitement like that is a relief from the monotony of peaceful warfare.

(Next Day)
Misfortunes never come singly! My only breeches being still wet this morning, Harris hung them up on a bush to dry. I girded a blanket round my loins and fastened it with a belt, like a rather long kilt. Of course, it would be at this very moment that, through the orchard, arrived a cavalcade consisting of Brigadier-General Kincaid-Smith (Commanding 25th Divisional Artillery), his Brigade Major, and the Staff Captain. I could not hide, so stood up and saluted with full ceremony. He asked me why I was dressed like that, and when I told him, he laughed good and hearty. He inspected our guns, billets and stables and was quite complimentary. I must say I was relieved when they had gone; though it was nice to meet him. He was an old-fashioned type, reminding me very much of Uncle Fred, from his leather gaiters to his flat cap worn without a hat spring; and above his walrus moustache twinkled the same blue eyes. Incidentally it was the only time I've ever seen a general of any kind on the battle-field, if you can call it that.

This afternoon a driver arrived from the wagon-line with a spare horse and a message asking that one of my gunners (a soccer pro) should go down the line to play for our brigade team in a match against a local A.S.C. unit.* So you see the peculiar sort of warfare we are engaged in!

30th Nov. A/112 Bde

Still at the detached section. It was freezing last night, and now a bitter wind is blowing. Feeling particularly hardy, I went out this morning, broke the ice on a small shell-hole and washed in the open in nothing but a pair of breeches. I am only just beginning to come to life again after ten minutes round a brazier of burning wood in this dugout. Our system of ventilation is a bit faulty (in fact there isn't any) and at the moment I am choking and weeping as if we had a tear-gas attack on our hands.

Yesterday, I went to Battalion HQ in Givenchy on Liaison Duty, and my telephonist was to follow a quarter of an hour later. An hour passed, but no telephonist. Wondering if he had got strafed on the way up, I walked back along the unused road from Givenchy Church to Windy Corner looking for him. At the time one of our machine-guns was letting off an occasional burst at nothing in particular.

Suddenly a voice from the roadside ditch, 'Is that you, Sir?' I said 'Yes', then 'Get down quick, Sir, there's a machine-gun firing up this road.' It turned out that he'd spent nearly an hour in the ditch thinking he was under fire! He was very relieved when I explained there was nothing to worry about.

I've had a letter from Mrs Robinson with a sketch showing where she has been told Geoffrey is buried. It is six or seven miles south of here, and I'll ride over there next fine

---

* Army Service Corps.

day as it is in our territory. His elder brother was killed on the same day at Loos, but his grave is now in no-man's-land, so I don't think I'll visit that one.

The Section of the line just north of us is held by the Portuguese, inevitably known to our chaps as the 'Pork and Beans'. They wear grey baggy uniforms and thin black boots, and their officers have a rather showy and be-medalled appearance. Somehow they don't look very tough soldiers, which is no doubt why they've been allotted to this quiet part of the line. But one feels it's jolly decent of them to be here at all, even though they are 'our oldest ally'. One thinks by contrast of another much greater nation whose troops might well have been here before now!

3rd December. A/112

I rode over yesterday to try to reach Robinson's grave but the Boche was on the strafe all round and, as walking through shells is an over-rated pastime, I've postponed my visit for another day.

Today I've been all day at the O.P. sniping Huns when-ever they moved, because one in a Hun sausage-balloon tried to be funny at my expense while I was walking to the O.P. It was the old trick. I had to pass a road junction in full view. Fortunately, I spotted a number of fresh shell-craters around it, and therefore took a short cut over the field about 50 yards to one side. As I came level with the road junction, a 5.9 burst right on it! I ducked down till the bits had whizzed by, made a suitable gesture towards the balloon and hastened my steps to the O.P.

Our O.P. is a concrete cell concealed in a ruined house, about twenty or thirty yards from the huge heap of rubble that was Givenchy Church. Naturally the Boche registers his field-guns on it, which gives us an interesting view of shells like our own bursting at close quarters. We sit and look out through a narrow split at the Boche trenches just two hundred yards away. Uncle Bill's telescope is very useful here. I've made a panorama sketch of the view, from the chimney of Marquillies Sugar Factory on our left round to the famous Railway Triangle of La Bassée on our right. Labelling the main features of the view with their appropriate map references will help other gunner officers who are new to the place.

The most interesting thing to be seen from here is a certain tree-stump about ten feet high that stands with several others just behind our front line. The first thing one notices is that it has quite a few bullet holes in it, yet the wood shows no sign of splitting. Closer inspection reveals a small door in the back of it, invisible to the Boche. It is in fact a steel reproduction, which has been substituted for the real tree-trunk, of which it is an exact copy. In it a man, arriving and leaving under cover of dark, might sit all day unseen within forty yards of the enemy front-line trench. What fun for him! At least that, I am told, was the original idea. But I don't think they use it any more. And looking at those bullet holes, one feels sorry for anyone who was inside when the trick was discovered. I would much prefer our concrete cell, cold though it is.

(Later)

Just returned to hear that we are moving tomorrow, I don't know where. Farewell to our orchard! Must get this off to you right away.

CHAPTER ELEVEN

Deep Winter at Bapaume

December 6th, 1917. A112 Brigade R.F.A.

On 4th we packed up and came south by train, and have gone into action west of Cambrai. After the tank battle ten days ago the Germans have hit back very hard. They broke through and succeeded in surrounding a Field Gun Battery. It fought to the end and was wiped out. So it seems we may be in for some pretty stiff fighting.

Our train journey down here was no picnic. At Bethune my job was to entrain the horses and mules, while another subaltern directed the loading of guns and weapons. The horses had to be run up ramps into trucks where they were tethered side by side. Sometimes, a nervous horse would protest vigorously, lashing out with its hoofs. One of the others would fall down in the scuffle, and all the rest have to be taken out to let it get up; and then we would start all over again.

But loading the horses was child's play compared with

the mules. Of these, some regarded our efforts with sullen suspicion and refused to move until dragged in by brute force and ropes; others rushed in headlong and began a general offensive against the other occupants of the truck; others again were light-hearted and skittish, kicked everything within reach, and got their legs tangled in the rails of the ramp. We eventually found that the best method for these awkward ones was to run them up and down the platform till they got excited, then throw a coat over their heads, and turn them round and round, as in Blind Man's Buff; and finally hit them over the nose and run them backwards into the truck. This method we found infallible even with the worst. By five in the evening the whole battery was on board, and we were off.

The afternoon had been quite mild and most of us were without greatcoats, but when darkness fell it began to freeze hard. We did our best to keep warm by huddling together in our doorless carriages, but were stiff and cold when at 2 a.m. we reached the deserted station of Boisleux-au-Mont and were told to off-load. A thorough search in the darkness produced only one old ramp. Unloading the horses by this means was a maddeningly slow process, in flurries of snow and a searing wind. For the guns and wagons the only unloading place was a platform in a siding just long enough to take one truck at a time. As there was no engine to shunt the trucks, we had to push them one by one, heavily loaded as they were, up the line and back over a set of points to the siding. We then discovered that the station staff at Bethune had wedged the wagon-wheels with wooden blocks, hammered into the floor of the trucks with six-inch nails; and of course all the ropes were like bars of iron from the intense frost. But somehow or other the job was done at last, and the chill rising sun found us marching through featureless snowy wastes towards our destination – the village of Courcelles.

Here the Camp Site allotted to us was on the exposed top of a ridge, where there was nothing but a few tents to give shelter from the wind. The water troughs had three inches of ice on them, but a pick-axe overcame that difficulty. Slowly we watered and fed the animals, found some wood for fires, boiled up some tea and gradually warmed ourselves by grooming the horses. When I tried to wash I found my sponge was frozen, and my efforts to bend it only resulted in breaking it in half. However the main thing is that the fire-wood supply has been secured for another twenty-four hours or so. By now we've almost forgotten the existence of the Germans, our immediate concern being with the struggle for survival in the open, under ten to twenty degrees of frost, and a cutting wind.

The poor horses droop patiently at their ropes, their blankets just keeping them alive. It's a good thing we've only clipped their legs and manes. The men are muffled in woollen balaclavas and leather jerkins. We have rigged up one or two canvas windscreens behind which fires are kept going, but these have to be put out by nightfall to avoid attracting bombers. I am wearing nearly everything I've got, but just cannot keep my feet warm.

December 14th

This icy weather so far shows little sign of a break, but we have settled in better now. The gun position is in front of a sunken road in which we have made some warm dugouts; but the wagon-lines are awful, with the men in tents. In places the mud is shin deep. It pours by day and freezes by night, and the penetrating wind never stops. Under their blankets, the horses have rapidly grown thick hairy coats and somehow manage to survive. Rations are poor – bully beef and army biscuits, often no bread; and with the Somme battlefield extending for twenty miles behind us, there is little chance at present of getting anything extra from shops, as we did at Ypres and Givenchy.

The Boche has been so venturesome that we've had to put a barbed wire screen twenty-five yards in front of the guns – just in case.

Some way in front of our gun position I've found a cross, made from a broken aeroplane propeller, at the head of a grave outlined with white painted stones. Round the propeller-hub is painted '2nd Lieut. J. G. Will. R.F.C.' He was the wing three-quarter known before the war as 'the flying Scot'. I heard he had been shot down some months ago, when this was enemy territory. The grave must have been made by Boche airmen – a curiously chivalrous act, for they can hardly have thought it likely that we would advance far enough to see it.*

Dec 20th. A/112 Brigade R.F.A. (in front of Bapaume)

Just to show you that we are not completely isolated from civilisation, I enclose with best wishes for a Happy Christmas a bottle of scent. I'm afraid some of it leaked into my pocket on the journey – and I hope the rest will not have done the same before it reaches you. If so, just remember that, as you so often say, it's the spirit rather than the gift itself that matters! I had to lorry-jump 30 miles west to Amiens to get it yesterday.

It was a fascinating journey – the first 20 miles of it right across the Somme battlefield to Albert [see plan, on page 192], where the Golden Virgin still leans down from her shattered spire.† We passed through two villages on the main road, which are household words by now, Le Sars and

---

* I was later told that Lieutenant Will had signalled 'Going home' to his pals, as he went down in flames.

† Damaged in 1915 and strengthened, it was said, by French engineers lest it should fall and (so ran the prophecy) involve the destiny of France in its ruin. A Hun shell brought it down the following spring, when the prophecy came within an ace of being fulfilled!

Pozières; and near Thiepval and Mouquet Farm; but of these literally not a trace remains, the sites being down to ground level and returned in all detail to their original dust and now overgrown with rank grass and weeds. Of Pozières nothing at all was left but one grey granite step by the road-side where the entrance of the church had been. A number of wrecked tanks still lay where they were abandoned, and a pair of chalky craters marked the remains of La Boiselle. There were many areas, particularly near the old front line, dotted with crops of white wooden crosses; I should think about a hundred or more to the acre. And how many others lie there unmarked? The low mound bearing the famous name of the Butte de Warlancourt has been fenced off by the French authorities with a notice-board urging the sacredness of the spot. Not inappropriately, its summit is crowned with three crosses.

I have spent the whole of today with my signaller sitting in a small shelter dug in the face of a grass-grown bank overlooking the Boche line several hundred yards away. There were 28 degrees of frost, a record even for this savagely cold winter. We have no means of keeping warm, as there is barely room to swing our arms. To avoid being seen we have to be in position before daylight, and only leave at dusk. By that time we are nearly dead with cold. My feet were sore to begin with, but later went numb, which was better; but we were fairly staggering on the way home. We have this joy-trip every fourth day. Thank God, it won't be my turn on Christmas Day.

December 28th

This Christmas was about the happiest I ever spent. At midnight on Christmas Eve we loosed off thirty rounds of H.E. at a Boche Battalion H.Q. – this by way of wishing them a Merry Christmas; but there was no reply. Early on Christmas morning all except the Sub on duty went to the front-line to give our greetings to the infantry. They complained of a machine-gun that had fired intermittently during the night from the Bird-Cage, a strong fortified post projecting into no-man's-land. So we rang the battery and plastered the spot with H.E. Then we found they were out of whisky – so sent them down a couple of bottles. All morning and afternoon messages of good wishes kept pouring in from other batteries and Headquarters, which we returned.

In the evening there was a grand dinner all round. The men got (from money raised by the officers and their families) a big feed of ham, potatoes, fresh cabbage and plum pudding, and each one a personal gift of half-lb. cake, two bars of chocolate, an orange, an apple, and a box of one hundred cigarettes – and a double issue of rum. Soon they were in full voice, both in their dugouts and in the open, and we had our health drunk in the Sergeants' Mess. After that we sat down, fifteen of us including guests, to the following Menu, all from Amiens (a sixty mile journey), and served on a clean table-cloth: Oysters; Tomato Soup; Herrings; Turkey with Baked Potatoes and Cauliflower; Sausages and Stuffing; Plum Pudding; Pate de fois gras, biscuits and cheese; Coffee; Fruit; and Chocolates. We also had ten bottles of champagne and some cigars.

Speeches and songs followed; and around midnight there was a spirited snow-fight in which Majors and subalterns fought indiscriminately. Then we went forward to Battalion H.Q., and serenaded the Colonel with 'Good King Wenceslas', while the snow lay round about deep and crisp and even; also a selection of other less respectable songs. After this some of our party had to assist each other back to the battery; but another Sub and I persuaded a Company Commander to let us go out into no-man's-land. He came with us and we moved stealthily out till we were within earshot of the Hun wire, where we sat for a while in a shell-hole. Presently we heard German voices, which was rather exciting. We wanted to sing them 'Stille nacht, Heilege nacht'; but the Company Commander took the view that however heilege our intentions might be, the nacht would probably not remain at all stille! So we bowed to his greater experience – after all, he's got to live with them – and returned to our own lines, for some more carol singing. And so to bed.

Yesterday I had a narrow squeak for a 'blighty'. We had been out trying to shoot rats with our revolvers, and came in to sit by the fire. One of the others, in unloading, dropped a round in the ashes under the fire, but we couldn't find it. A minute later there was a loud bang and the bullet skimmed my boot leaving a scar on the leather. An inch lower, and I might have been en route for home in a couple of days from now. But no such luck!

CHAPTER TWELVE

Waiting

January 1st, 1918. A/112 Brigade R.F.A.
In the ice-box O.P. again, an odd place to start the New Year. But here at least there is time to write. We hear that in the very near future the Boche may come over and look us up in quite a big way. I am due for liaison with the infantry on the expected morning, and shall be carrying my knobkerrie and revolver with my pockets full of ammunition, ready to settle someone's hash. My job is to hang around with the infantry and direct the fire of four batteries in whatever way will help them most. But it's a novelty to us to be on the defensive.

We were discussing in the Mess the other day how many Germans we could rightly claim to have killed. It doesn't seem nearly enough. We agreed that since the war had dragged on so long, the sides must be fairly evenly matched – British, French and Russians vs. Germans and Austrians. Never mind the rest. That being so, if every man on one side killed just one man on the other side, no one would be left, and the war would be over. Therefore we concluded that on average we had killed much less than one German each, which seems a very poor result for so much effort.

Yet we gunners must have killed many in our barrages at Ypres. To take only once instance that I can be sure about, the local attack in Hannebeek Wood that I flattened out on my last day in the Salient must have accounted for fifty or more Germans killed. But of course I must share these amongst all our gunners that fired the guns, the drivers that brought up the ammunition, the A.S.C. that feed us, the line of communication troops that enable us to move, the Generals and their staffs that direct our operations, and lastly but most important of all the P.B.I. that hold the line while we fire over their heads. But it is frustrating that so few of us can say – I killed one of the enemy. Here, in this peaceful sector, we have not even had a chance to try.

At last the thaw seems to have come, temporarily at least, and the mud has a very gluey consistency. We are back on the old rations again. Army biscuits more often than bread; tea and sugar in the same sand-bag separated by a string knotted round its waist, so that the two only inter-mingle to a moderate extent. I like sugar in my tea, but care less for dry tea leaves in my sugar. Our mess cook has recently returned from a course on cookery. Main result is that the bully-beef rissoles are oblong instead of round.

Again and again I am struck by the impersonality of this war. Here we sit, and I gaze through my glasses at the bare slopes opposite. The only sign of war is the belts of rusty barbed wire of the Hindenburg Line. Is there anyone there? Not a sign of it. And this bit opposite us is only a tiny piece in a line nearly 400 miles long from Switzerland to the Channel. 400 miles. What a siege! You would think it would be impossible to man such a length of line, let alone man it so effectively that the other side can't break through. Yet no one sees anyone opposite them . . .

(That is not strictly correct. I have just spotted two Boches, carrying what looks like a Dixie of food along a section of open road near Pronville. A nice dinner of hot stew for someone. Miller here says he can't stop his mouth watering!)

We had our chance here in November. The general opinion is that the break-through by tanks into the back areas at Cambrai could have led to the rolling up of the whole German line by taking it in the rear if only it had been properly followed up. But apparently the Boches were not the only ones who turned out to be unprepared. Now, that chance having been missed, the initiative has gone over to them, because they have been enormously re-inforced with troops from the Eastern front following Russia's collapse. It's their big chance to win the war before the Yanks join us.

January 5th – in the ice-box O.P.
All set for a bit of mischief today. The other Subs have confirmed my observation that shortly after 12.30 p.m. each day, those Boche mess orderlies, with an N.C.O. in attendance, carry a large Dixie down the road and disappear behind a clump of bushes. They are visible for eighteen seconds only, but that is just long enough.

The centre section know what is afoot. I have bracketed the road in three rounds of H.E. from Durney's gun; and then swinging off target, fired two rounds of shrapnel to check the height of the burst. All this was done at ten minute intervals, so as to give an impression of random shots, testing a gun. Lindfield's gun is now laid on the same spot just short of the bushes. The same gunner has been setting the fuses to eliminate any personal error. Time of flight is fifteen seconds, so allowing two seconds from my order to fire in the O.P. to the pulling of the triggers, we may just be in time to catch them before they pass behind the bushes. Two hours to go . . .

(Later) Well, it's done now.

At 12.25 p.m., Miller reported 'Both guns ready and set, Sir', and then passed my order 'Stand by to fire in five minutes' time'.

By 12.30 p.m., through binoculars, I was watching the chalky road where it shone white and deserted in the wintry sunlight. The minutes dragged by. Miller whispered down the telephone to make sure the battery telephonist was listening.

Suddenly three figures appeared on the road. I paused a second just to make sure, then ordered 'Fire!'

'Fire!' said Miller, and

'Both guns fired, Sir.'

A faint double thump confirmed it, followed by the fading swish of the shells as they sped towards the target.

Down the open road walked the Boches with their load of stew. I lowered the glasses to give my eyes a rest; then looked again. Two cotton-wool puffs appeared right above the target, and there on the road by the bushes sprawled three motionless figures. Others presently emerged and gathered round, making a tempting target, but somehow I felt we'd done enough.

'We'll leave them to clear up the mess,' I said. 'Pass the word to stand down. Both shots bang on target. Well done, Centre Section.'

Ten minutes later came retribution; about a dozen crumps much too close for comfort; one only a few yards off which shook us up and nearly brought the roof in. We have been warned. Evidently they know roughly where this O.P. is, in spite of our efforts to avoid being seen entering and leaving.

An ambush is a cold-blooded affair, but they've tried to

get me several times, so it's fair enough. And it's right to show the Boche we are here and ready to hit him whenever we have the chance. Then if he does attack, he will know he is walking into trouble – and perhaps hesitate a little.

January 13th. A/112 Bde. Near Morchies

The day forecast for the expected attack has passed off without incident. I spent most of the night with the colonel of the battalion out in no-man's-land, where extensive wiring was going on. They were screwing in steel corkscrew stakes, and spreading out springy concertina wire, which follows you around if you get caught in it. The Hun was very restive, sending up Verey lights and searching the ground with his machine-guns; and at intervals we were on our faces in the mud with bullets hissing just overhead. Two casualties. We returned at 4am, half frozen and coated with yellow clay from head to foot.

The thaw has come now, and it's been raining for two days. Most of our dugouts are flooded; the trenches falling in, and in places 2ft deep in water and mud. No doubt the Hun is in the same state, as no shells are coming over; and we are too busy and miserable to shell him.

There's one bit of really good news. I've just heard that my pay is to go up to 10/6 a day or £192 a year! So with field allowance, etc. as long as I'm out here, I'll be getting nearly £250 a year.

January 21st. A/112 R.F.A. In front of Bapaume

We've been busy this week building a proper O.P. in the support trench, where we shall now be much more comfortable in bad weather. This has meant getting a lot of material to a forward site which is in full view of the enemy – such as duckboards, corrugated-iron, small elephant-irons, planks, sandbags and rolls of camouflage netting. It would have been a frightful sweat carrying it all up the communication trenches, so I decided to take it there on a G.S. Wagon in the dark.

We chose a cloudy night and, carrying two improvised bridges, got over all the intervening trenches, and came to a halt at the support trench, which was on the crest of the slope. We were all gathered round the wagon, piled high like a removal van, and a squad of the men were starting to unload, when suddenly the full moon threw its dazzling searchlight on us. I shouted 'Don't move. Wait for it.' And there we all stood motionless – and I expect praying hard. Anyway within half a minute the clouds closed up again and hid us; and we heaved the stuff on the ground in record time, and got the wagon away without a shot being fired. Fritz was presumably asleep.

The rest was easier. Keeping a wary eye on the clouds, we completed all the work that was required above ground. Next morning at daybreak, I crawled out in front of the trench and checked over the camouflage, so that from the Boche lines no one could see that there had been any change in the appearance of the parapet. This brought some protests from our gunners who thought the enemy were nearer than they really are. But we have been too safe in this cushy area, and I think you need to practise taking occasional risks or you become too trench-minded.

When it was all done, we had a cosy dugout for four, with seats, a dry duckboard floor, a fire-place with a non-smoking flue, and a wind-proof door. It gives the best possible view of the German Front Line; and what's more, it's splinter-proof.

Jaunts of this sort have helped me in getting to know the men of the Centre Section individually. They have a wonderful spirit and loyalty to each other, and a good-humoured endurance that seemingly nothing can break down. They strengthen me; and now and then show me con-sideration in a way that warms the heart.

Our Major, Swinton, has gone to the wagon-line, and Captain Stanley Jones is now permanently in charge of the gun position. This change is probably to give him more front line experience, as so far he has been almost always at the wagon-lines. He is a very nice chap, amusing, and I would think as cool as a cucumber if he was in a hot spot. He asked me to share his dug-out, and I am very happy to be in with him. I have built a little fireplace against the wall between our bunks, and in the morning I can light it from my bed, so that the place is beautifully warm by the time we have to get up. His servant calls us with early morning tea; but unfortunately no papers; so I've lent him *Pickwick Papers* which he reads in bed, quietly shaking with laughter.

We've had a confidential message from HQ that we shall be 'pushed' before long, and that we are to remain here till that happens. It can't be so very confidential as the newspapers are saying the same thing and, what's more, are naming the Quéant sector, opposite us, as being the centre of the coming attack. So now we know. Well, he'll get a bloody nose when he comes!

February 7th

My two guns have been moved to Morchies, a ruined village ¾ mile from the main battery position, so that they can be fired at close range down a valley up which the Boche will advance if he penetrates our front line. These two guns don't fire much at present, and I come over for duty at the battery every day, and go back to sleep at the detached section by night.

On the way, I have to pass through seven belts of barbed wire comprising the Reserve Line. Of course it would happen that my first return trip was made on a pitch-black night, and my torch battery was out. I walked gingerly across the field, managing somehow to avoid the shell-holes but my first contact with the wire was when I tripped and fell spread-eagled on the outer apron of it! Groping my way along it I found the gap in the first and then the second belts, but the third gap was nowhere to be found, and by the time I had finished looking for it, I had lost my whereabouts completely. Finally, I just had to worm my way under the next four belts till I got through, torn and bleeding – and so got home to my dugout where Harris was waiting for me. He's got a good deal of darning and mending to do! And I've now marked my zigzag route through the wire with a white tape.

Harris has made my dug-out a real home from home. From ammunition boxes collected from a heavy howitzer section, he has made a bedstead, table and stool – and a spring mattress from the springs of the 9.2 howitzer charge boxes. He has built a brick fire-place in which there is always a roaring log-fire, scrounged a huge copper tub from one of the ruined houses for my hot bath, and made a carpet of empty sand-bags to cover the floor; and even found four sheets of glass and made a window. It is now not so much a dug-out as a fortified bed-sitting room – and a triumph of initiative and devotion on his part.

I forgot to tell you that when we came to this sector, two months ago, Captain Jones got me a charger that had belonged to an officer in another battery who was wounded. She is called 'Fly', an awful name I think, but she is far better than Molly, who was really too small for my weight. Fly is a powerful chestnut mare, full of spirit, and I have bribed my way into her affections with the cube-sugar we can get out here. I have ridden her very little because of being all the time at the battery position, but now that the snow has gone I can ride her at times, and she's a real fizzer. The other day I had her brought up from the wagon-line and rode her back the four or five miles on my own. This is all open country like Salisbury Plain, and when she felt the grass underfoot and saw the open spaces in front she just went like the wind. It was a new experience for me, and I could do with lots more of it. In our gallop, we came to a deep sunken road, which still held several feet of drifted snow. I tried to put her down the bank into it, but she absolutely refused to budge. So I threw the reins on her neck to see what she would do; and sure enough, she walked along the edge for a couple of hundred yards till she found a place where it was safe to cross; and through it she went, with no guidance from me, which I think shows real intelligence. Anyway she's the first horse of my own that I'm really thrilled to have and from now on nothing can be too good for her.

February 20th. A/112 R.F.A.
We came out of the line on 14th February, and for the past week have been doing intensive training at Meaulte, near Albert, to the west of the old Somme battlefield.

Training is a frightful sweat. We spend all day at gun-drill, mounted battery-drill, and even infantry drill, all in preparation for open fighting once again. We've almost forgotten it, being so used to the 'siege warfare' conditions of the past year. But it's been easy for me to recollect the Woolwich patter of riding drill and infantry drill, and to put my chaps through their paces at a level of smartness that they've probably never known before. Anyhow they're keen all right and have taken the rigorous training dished out to them in a good spirit. The guns, vehicles, harness and even the horses and mules have taken on a new smartness. Our efforts have been watched by Col. Sarson, Brig. Gen. Kincaid-Smith, and other brass-hats; and we have all done our best to be a credit to Jones, as rumour has it that he may be promoted to Major and given command of the battery – and that we should all like.

I had an interesting talk with Sgt. Durney the other day, when I asked him whether the men didn't get utterly fed-up at living in such squalid conditions in mouldy dugouts, and eating monotonous food. Wasn't their apparent cheerfulness just put on as a show? But he tells me the squalid side of the war just doesn't matter to them at all, so long as they have their own friends with them, and are fairly treated by their officers and N.C.O.s. What does make them wild is to get about 2/6 a day out here and read of Clydeside dockers and South Wales miners, who get at least five times as much, striking and holding up the docks and war production to demand still higher pay. They really are savage about that.

February 27th. A/112. Meaulte

We've been awfully fed up, because in spite of all our efforts to smarten up, Jones was told that A/112 was not nearly smart enough; and it was hinted that unless we pulled our socks up, there would be no question of promotion for him. When he told us this there was general gloom, not unmixed with indignation at the brass-hats, who seem to do nothing but criticise. But we stuck at it and put on the pressure; and anyone in my section who showed any signs of slacking has had it in the neck good and hearty.

Our training ends tomorrow – and now the full low cunning of the brass-hats stands revealed. A/112 Battery has been selected for a special job, as being the smartest battery in the 25th Division! Our three two-gun sections are now to become mobile anti-tank guns, operating independently of other artillery, with power to commandeer anyone else's ammunition wherever we are. When I asked where do we go and what do we do, the reply was simple. 'The Boche are expected to attack with tanks. These must be destroyed. You are each responsible for a thousand-yard-wide sector of the front. How you do it is entirely up to you.' It was implied that after the battle decorations would be dished out to any survivors. (Hollow laughter from us three Subs!)

Now that this has become known to the men, there is

tremendous keenness. Rivalry between the three sections is almost reaching the dimension of a feud.

Meanwhile I have been told provisionally that I am due for leave on 6th March. I felt bound to offer to defer this in view of the impending attack and the new job assigned to me; but they now think the attack won't come before the end of March, and I'll be back well before then.

March 3rd. A/112 – 'Special service section!'

We've been very busy preparing for our special job. With Sgts. Durney and Lindfield, I've made an exhaustive inspection of our sector, deciding on the best points to shoot from and how best to approach them, and where to put reserve dumps of ammunition. Then each gun crew has been taken round and every single man shown what to do, as these guns will have to go on working even if there are only two junior gunners left to work them. They also know how to destroy the guns as a last resort. So we've been practising 'action in the open' till it's as slick as can be; and we have brought up our horses and limbers and stabled them in some ruined buildings behind the gun position. The limbers are loaded with our minimum kit and two days' rations and water.

I've taken the men over the approach route, where they drive at a gallop through belts of wire and across filled-in bits of trench, and we've levelled out the track where necessary for this purpose.

On the first of these 'death-or-glory' drives, a gunner failed to secure the back of a limber properly, and when we reached our action position it was found that 18 rounds of ammunition were missing. It was a very red-faced gun crew that went back over the course and succeeded in recovering all the missing rounds. That won't happen again.

I've also laid on practical tests. Without giving us previous warning, Infantry H.Q. 'phone through the 'Tanks' signal about 5 or 6 a.m. Immediately a trumpet is sounded at the battery, we jump up and dress, horses are harnessed and hooked in, and I lead my section at a gallop about a mile and a half to the rendezvous, under cover near the front line. Here an infantry officer is waiting, watch-in-hand, to telephone our time of arrival to H.Q. Our best time to date is four minutes to be ready to move off, and eight minutes to get to the rendezvous. So far I'm glad to say the Centre Section has never failed to be the first of the three to move off.

It is a great thrill and privilege to be chosen for this job. I do at least feel that I have made the grade as a field-gunner; and we are all ready for whatever may come.*

I've just heard from Clifton that George Paton, who was in our house, was killed in December and has got a posthumous V.C. He was a Captain in the Coldstream Guards and already had an M.C. At school he was a bit of a dandy, with a gay sense of humour, taking nothing seriously – not even his own life, it seems.

* Until I left them for the last time, it was the proud boast of Centre Section that no one had equalled our record time for the turn-out. We had our tails up in those days: the only fly in the ointment was (as usual) the Hun who, when he did eventually come over, came without a single tank!

CHAPTER THIRTEEN

'Fight on to the End'

On 6 March 1918, I went on a fortnight's leave. It was quiet and refreshing, and little more need be said about it. On my last night I sat in the stalls of the Hippodrome enchanted by the swing of the music and the chorus girls' legs. Shirley Kellogg, with her basket of tulips, swayed down the illuminated 'Joy-Plank', singing

> Tew-lip Time, Tew-lip Time,
> That's the time for me!

I was one of the lucky ones to whom she threw a tulip. Unfortunately I was so fascinated by the auburn hair in her arm-pits that I dropped the catch . . .

Next morning I faced the leave-train with a heart of lead, and a strong presentiment that this third journey out would be my last. The sun was shining as I settled into my corner seat, but that only served to increase my depression at leaving London where life looked so good. My imagination pictured with most unwelcome realism the last stand of an 18-pounder gun against advancing German tanks. Fortunately there was no one to see me off; that would have made it worse. As the crowded leave-train pulled slowly out of Waterloo, and I 'cast one longing lingering look behind' for some little concrete thing to remember London by, my gaze fastened on a set of enamel signs on a low wall at the side of the track, advertising Petter Oil Engines. It was as if I asked them to remember me when I came no more that way. Thank God for the cheerful soul in the opposite seat whose determination to dispel his hangover with a flask of brandy helped at last to chase away my gloom.*

Next morning, across the Channel – to be exact, at 4.43 a.m. on 21 March 1918 – all Hell was let loose . . .

It is not my purpose to describe the final German offensive, so fully portrayed by others. On a front of 40 miles, over three-quarters of a million Germans, armed as never before, pulverised and then set upon 300,000 British. Sir Winston Churchill in his book on the Great War called it 'without exception the greatest onslaught in the history of the World'. And I will leave it at that.†

---

* Fate sometimes overdoes things. In later life, it decreed that I was to pass these same advertisements twice daily for years on end on my way to a job in London, till the monotony of the journey might almost have made me sick of the sight of them. But I never quite forgot what they had once meant to me.

† From the Sensée River to the Oise, on a front of 40 miles, the Germans launched simultaneously thirty-seven divisions of infantry, covered by 6,000 guns. They held in close support nearly thirty further divisions. On the same front the British line of battle was held by seventeen divisions and 2,500 guns, with five divisions in support. In all the Germans had marshalled and set in motion rather more than three-quarters of a million men against 300,000 British. Over the two ten-mile sectors lying to the north and south of the salient, in which

On the evening of 21 March, after a calm channel crossing, I sat at dinner in the Officers' Club at Boulogne. Presently we were joined by a gunner captain who casually remarked, 'I've heard a rumour that there's something doing up the line.' We pricked up our ears. I wanted to get to the battery at once, especially in view of our anti-tank role. But there was no train to the Bapaume area before next morning, and no one else was worrying much about it. The general feeling was that even if this should turn out to be the long-heralded German push, all preparations had been made to deal with it weeks ago.

And so, on the morning of 22 March, the returning leave train moved out from Boulogne at a dignified speed. It turned out to be the slowest journey of my life – two days and a night to cover roughly sixty miles to Achiet-le-Petit, a few miles short of Bapaume.* At that point we were detrained, and all the officers were formed up in two ranks by an elderly colonel and instructed that they were to return by another train to Doullens 'to be re-distributed'. With some misgivings they marched off, but I dodged behind a railway wagon. I knew that somewhere in front of Bapaume A/112 must be up to their necks in the battle. They would be needing me. God knows I needed them! So I set off on foot to find them.

Thus it was that in gathering dusk I returned alone to Achiet-le-Petit, and there by the merest chance noticed a gateway bearing our divisional sign, the Red Horseshoe. And what should it be but the very headquarters of the

the 9th Division stood, the density of the enemy's formation provided an assaulting division for every thousand yards of ground, attaining the superiority of four to one.

* I had no map of the back areas, and it has always been a mystery to me where we could have got to during those two days of aimless railway travel, as the front line was hardly more than fifty miles from Boulogne!

25th Division. I reported at once to the brigade major of the Divisional Artillery, got my first meal for two days and lay down to sleep on the wooden floor of a hut, the only place I could find.

Early next morning, 24 March, as no one seemed to know where A/112 might be, I set out with my rucksack on my back, to look for the battery. I walked through Achiet-le-Grand and Bihucourt, past Grevillers and across the Bapaume–Albert road. On these roads, all traffic was moving steadily away from the front line, an ominous spectacle. South of Bapaume, I met a battery 'retiring' out of action, and a subaltern told me that there were no guns further forward, that all batteries had already retired westwards.

By this time the sun was blazing hot and I was getting tired slogging along in my 'British Warm' overcoat. My rucksack weighed a ton and I longed for a horse. However, I reluctantly turned westwards, looking eagerly for any sign of the Red Horseshoe. I felt uneasy about this: as an officer who had disobeyed instructions and was now moving away from the fighting line without his unit, I might have to answer some very awkward questions. After a couple of miles I reached Butte de Warlencourt and, still finding no sign of any guns, I concluded with fury that the subaltern had been talking through his hat, and turned eastwards again.

By now the roadway was crowded with traffic: signal companies, pioneers, Chinese labour battalions, pigeon units, A.S.C. wagons, D.A.C. wagons, motor lorries, ambulances, staff cars, every kind of vehicle and men, all trekking westwards. Such a crowd that I had to walk on the verge to make headway against them.

Two hours and several miles further forward, the stream of vehicles thinned, occasional shells fell, and the sound of guns indicated that the fighting was not far off.

And now down the roads and tracks the wounded came flocking, many supporting each other, some drenched in blood and hardly able to totter, some of the less-seriously wounded wheeling a badly smashed pal, groaning on a stretcher. Others with no apparent injuries reeled along, laughing or crying, with no idea of who, where or why they were. By the roadside an advanced dressing station was doing its best to cope with this flood of casualties; and I thought it as well to get a field-dressing from them.

It all seemed as unreal as a dream: that I should be pressing on towards the front line, immaculate in high-polished boots, new British Warm, soft cap and walking stick, against this stream of battle-stained men, so intent on getting away from it all. The fact that they had been able to walk this far showed that the fighting was near, yet there was still no sign of my own, or any other artillery. Indeed I began to wonder if our brigade had moved to some other part of the line; or even whether it had already been over-run by the enemy's advance. If so, what on earth was I to do?

Then I looked round and saw just behind me a wagon loaded with forage, and riding alongside it our own battery Quartermaster Sergeant! Heaving that accursed rucksack on to the wagon, I hailed him with delight. But he had bad news. Six men had been killed. Major Swinton and a number of others had been wounded and evacuated and Captain Jones had not yet returned from leave. One subaltern had gone raving mad and was last seen brandishing a rifle and striding forward alone towards the advancing enemy. He then told me my groom had died of his wounds, my kit had been blown up and Fly had bolted and disappeared. The battery was now being run by the two remaining Subs, Nurcombe and Wheeler, and on this fourth day of the battle everyone was utterly worn out.

I was no use to anyone without a horse and told the

QM that if nothing else, I'd have to take one from a wagon-team. He thought for a moment and then offered me his spare mount, with the warning that the beast was stone-blind in one eye. My reply was that as long it had four legs, it would suit me. He also gave me a water bottle and said he'd try and get me a tin hat and gas-mask.

The battery came rumbling by and I was soon mounted on the QM's horse. It turned out to be a steady old thing (trust the QM!), impervious to war's alarms and able to see just as well with one eye as with two. Durney and Lindfield and the Centre Section seemed to be in good heart, but before I could say much to them, Colonel Sarson appeared and took me off to find a new position for the guns.

As soon as this was decided, I returned to the battery and at Nurcombe's suggestion (he being a few weeks senior to me) took charge for a while and brought the guns into action behind the village of Thilloy. But before we had fired a round we were suddenly ordered to another position a mile away, south of Grevillers. It turned out to be a very awkward site, in a field full of shell-holes; and darkness had fallen by the time we had manhandled the last of our 18-pounders into position. Retreats are apt to be confused affairs and presumably the German advance seemed likely to encircle Bapaume in the next few hours. At any rate, a messenger soon arrived with written instructions for A/112 to pull out yet again and take the road through Miraumont to Achiet-le-Petit and to be there by sunrise.

So we set to work to extricate the guns from that field, and before long we were on the road through Grevillers, our way dimly illuminated by the rising moon, and the lurid glow of smoke and fire from Bapaume on our right. Moving along the road with us were batches of our infantry, who seemed to have little or no idea of where they were going or what was happening. They had obviously suffered terrible losses and we didn't know if there was any organised infantry defence line left between us and the advancing enemy. I was riding along in front of the battery when two rifle shots cracked out in the darkness, the bullets hitting a motor lorry beside me. Our battery sergeant major let fly in a language all his own, whereupon chastened voices came back at us from the darkness. It appeared that two of our own infantry had mistaken us for German cavalry!

As we neared Irles, our progress grew slower and slower, and finally ceased altogether. The ground at either side of the road, being old battlefield, was impassable. The stoppage was complete. Motor vehicle engines were switched off and orders were passed down to extinguish all lights, even cigarettes. It transpired that there was an eight-mile block of traffic from Achiet-le-Petit through Miraumont and nearly back to Bapaume; and when the Boche entered Bapaume late that evening, there had been nothing between him and the tail of our helpless column half a mile away except a BEF canteen, stocked full of whisky. In effect, however, this proved to be a most power-ful rear-guard and, although we were jammed on that road from ten at night until seven the next morning, we remained unmolested throughout. The Hun even missed a wonderful opportunity of shooting us up from the air in the first hour of daylight before we were once more on the move.

But for us, trapped on that road, it was a sleepless night. A keen frost made our plight worse, for many of the men had lost their greatcoats in the confusion of battle. I tried to sleep leaning against a wagon but the cold was so intense that sleep was impossible. Accordingly, I handed over my horse and set off up the road to try and find out the cause of the hold-up.

Through Miraumont the traffic was solid, and so it was for at least a mile further on. Then I saw, sandwiched between two motor lorries, a Rolls-Royce with a flag on the bonnet. Inside, grim and silent, sat some top brass. From their very presence in our midst, and their impassive set faces, it was obvious that everything possible was being done to clear the road; and that was what I had come to find out. This was also confirmed by a military policeman, who insisted on my taking a swig from his water bottle. It was full of neat whisky.

Thus fortified, I made my way back to the battery and, against the icy steel rim of a gun wheel, wrote a letter in large straggly handwriting:

3 a.m., March 25th. Written by moonlight. Can't show a light

As you may have heard, the battery has been in action day and night for four days now, and we are absolutely dead beat. The Hun has poured over, at times with odds of ten to one, and although he has lost fearfully (about 200,000 it is rumoured) he has pressed us right back beyond B—,* and trench warfare has become open warfare. Our infantry fought to the end, and have had 95 per cent casualties. The Hun sometimes got within 500 yards of our guns but we mowed them down like cutting corn. We have been almost without food and drink and sleep all the time, and fighting throughout, though my battery has not suffered too badly.

Our major and second-in-command are wounded[†] and three of us subalterns are running the battery. The horses are absolutely done. I have lost all my kit to the Hun except what I stand in. Have neither gas-mask, revolver nor tin-hat, so hope they would [not] gas us.

We are dazed for lack of sleep and with the firing, but manage to keep our peckers up somehow. At the moment

---

* Bapaume.
[†] Our second-in-command, Captain Jones, was in fact on leave; but by then I was getting a little confused.

The Somme Battlefield, 1918

0 miles 6

Approximate position of German advance, as on the dates shown

My search for the battery (Miraumont to Bancourt)

Line of retirement of A Battery, 112 Brigade R.F.A.

Arras

Beaumetz

Boisleux-au-Mont

March 28th

March 24th

Croisilles

Hindenburg Line on March 21st

Quéant

Bullecourt

Bienvillers

Ayette

Courcelles

Ervillers

Lagnicourt

Vaulx

A/112

Morchies

Foncquevillers

Gommecourt

Bucquoy

Achiet-le-Grand

Bihucourt

Beugnâtre

Beugny

Hébuterne

Achiet

Bapaume

Frémicourt

Puisieux

Grévillers

Thilloy

Bancourt

Colincamps

Miraumont

Irles

A/112

Mailly-Maillet

March 28th

Le Sars

Butte de Warlencourt

March 24th

Thiepval

Ovillers

Pozières

Longueval

Contalmaison

La Boiselle

Combles

Albert

Fricourt

Méaulte

Péronne

River Ancre

Bray-sur-Somme

River Somme

Herbécourt

Map taken from the original drawn by the author

we are withdrawing, but the road is blocked, and I hope the Boche won't catch us.

I don't know if I will be able to post this. Don't expect regular letters, it's imposs. I was mistaken for a Boche tonight and fired at, but missed. Am quite safe so far, though rather down. I expect we'll stop him soon. Hot weather in day, cold at night. Love from H.

'*Gallo canente, spes redit*',* sang the poet. As the sun rose, so did our spirits. And had any cock crowed, the QM's hands would doubtless have been round its neck in no time. As it was, he produced some army biscuits, and shared them out amongst those whose pockets were empty. Having had nothing for twenty-four hours, I was glad to make my breakfast off one. But what raised the men's spirits more than anything else was that with the cover of darkness gone, they could light up and smoke. Most of them produced Corona cigars that they flashed about, band and all, with the greatest relish and their own version of High Society back-chat, which made us all laugh.† The cigars had obviously come from the Bapaume canteen; but how or when I had no idea. The QM's staff were not lacking in initiative and the horses pulling the battery mess-cart probably knew something. All I know is that almost every man in the battery had half a dozen in his pocket, and felt all the better for it. The horses, on the other hand, were badly short of food and water, and were beginning to look thin. All they could have was a drink of shell-hole water out of their drivers' tin hats.

Impatient to be moving, I walked a little way up the

* 'The cock crowing, hope returns'
† 'I do 'ope we shan't miss Ascot this year, old boy. You're goin' of course?'
'Not bloody likely, old chap. I reckon Jerry will get there first!'

column. Suddenly a horse whinnied. I turned, and there was my beloved mount, Fly, asking for her sugar. She had been pressed into service as lead-horse of a gun-team in another battery. They told me they had found her running loose; and pretty worn out she looked, reduced to a shadow through lack of food and water. But after some forceful discussion with the officer in charge, I got her back; and she carried me stout-heartedly for the remaining days of my service.

War is full of surprises. Poking around among some ruined huts by the roadside (they were in fact a recently evacuated dressing station, and still smelled strongly of iodine and blood) I found, of all things, a violin. One string was broken, but the bow was good; and in the silence of the hut I quietly played a few bars of 'Chanson Triste' in memory of its late owner, whoever he might have been.

During my midnight walk up the traffic block, I had not noticed any of the other batteries of our brigade, and began to wonder where they could be located in all that confusion. But now as we rumbled wearily along, a solitary figure came into view, standing pensively on a mound of rubble by the roadside and watching the column go by. As we came nearer I saw the red hat-band and gold braid of high rank, and guessed him to be Major-General Bainbridge, our divisional commander. He stood there in the sunshine, quite alone, scanning the faces of the men as they passed by. It was not the moment to call on the battery for an 'eyes left' – most of them were half asleep in the saddle – but I felt that something ought to be done, if only as a gesture of sympathy; for even generals are human, and he must have been a very worried man. So I saluted, and as cheerfully as possible said, 'Good morning, Sir. Have you seen anything of the 112th Brigade? We are A Battery.'

'And how are things with you?' he asked, coming down

off his mound of rubble and patting Fly's neck. 'We'll be all right, Sir,' I replied, 'if we can get some food and ammunition.' His smile was heart-warming as he directed me down the road and called out 'Good luck!' I gratefully saluted, wheeled Fly round and rode on to pick up my place in the column. Half a mile further on we found the scattered units of the Brigade assembling in a big field with water troughs laid on. We hurriedly watered the horses and collected our share of the ammunition, though far less than we wanted. Colonel Sarson then sent us back to Miraumont to go into action near Beauregard Dovecote, and afterwards retire on Puisieux if necessary. An hour later, we were in position and ready to receive the Germans as soon as they should appear over the skyline on the other side of the valley.

At 10 a.m. heavy machine-gun fire was heard coming from the ridge, and a few remnants of our infantry appeared, falling back towards us. A quarter of an hour later we could see small parties of Huns coming on to the ridge. We started in on them with shrapnel at about 1,500 yards' range, saw them halt and go to ground. Nurcombe was by now more rested and we discussed what to do. We decided to give the enemy another dose if they resumed their advance and then fall back to Puisieux as ordered. Presently, seeing some movement opposite, we were just about to open fire when a messenger rode up with a written order to retire via Achiet-le-Petit. Consternation! This meant advancing along two miles of the Ancre valley road, by now within machine-gun range of the Boche. This fact was probably not known when the order was dispatched. We were tempted to ignore this message as no reason was given for reversing the original instructions. However, Nurcombe's decision was that we should comply if at all possible. We were both uneasily aware that we might shortly be re-enacting the Charge of the Light Brigade, as a result of a similar misunderstanding. But the decision was taken, and the sooner we went through with it the better. So we pulled out from the gun position and trotted forward down the hill into Miraumont, which was already under casual shell-fire.

As soon as we took the valley road to Achiet-le-Petit, machine guns opened up on us. Their long-range fire was inaccurate, but unpleasant enough, and we urged our weary teams into a shambling gallop. As we passed along the valley we appeared to come under fire from a heavy Howitzer as, one by one, the arched culverts in the adjoining embankments of the Amiens–Arras railway line blew up with tremendous explosions, bringing lumps of concrete and steel tumbling down around us. With the drivers crouching low in the saddle, the horses redoubled their efforts and were nearly at their last gasp when we rattled into Achiet and pulled up for a breather. Several of the horses had been hit but to our surprise there were no other casualties from our 'death or glory' ride. (Later we heard that the railway had been prepared for demolition by our Engineers and it was they who were blowing it up at the last moment. But by then we were rather beyond caring who blew us up.)

At Achiet a guide met the battery, and brought us across country to Bucquoy. On the way, we passed an old line of trenches with several belts of rusty wire in front of them, manned by fresh reserves of infantry with plenty of ammunition, so we knew that a stand was to be made on that line at last. At Bucquoy we found some food, ammunition and forage. Quickly we replenished the limbers and moved off at once to Puisieux, which we entered in the early afternoon. It was good to find that the German advance had not yet reached it. Here at last we came upon a desperately needed supply of drinking water. It was a well in a garden, and the bucket and rope made watering the horses a slow process; but we moved in among the ruins, and in spite of occasional shells, loosened the horses' girths and let them drink their fill.

It was evening before we had finished and pulled out on to the Gommecourt road, so about two miles further on we led the battery into a side-track, and settled down for the night. As far as we knew there was nothing between us and the Boche and we made our arrangements accordingly. The guns were brought into position facing the enemy, my two Centre Section 18-pounders side by side in the roadway. Shrapnel shells with zero fuses were stacked by the guns, and the guns were loaded. An outpost was stationed under cover with a trip-wire across the road; the two roadway guns were manned by two men each, and the others slept by their guns. We dared not unharness the horses; they just lay down in their tracks and went to sleep, quite worn out. Their drivers snuggled up against them and they, too, slept soundly for the first time for four nights.

We three subalterns found a brazier, collected some wood and spent the night huddled together at the top of the steps of a deep dug-out built during the first battle of the Somme. Owing to the choking smoke and the need for continually adding fuel, we got little sleep; but it was as well for us to be wakeful, and better to be kippered than frozen. It was a good thing that we were undisturbed that night, for the men took a lot of waking next morning. Some even had to be rolled about on the ground before they came out of their stupor. As dawn came up we moved off again and passed through Gommecourt to Foncquevillers, where we received instructions to make for Hébuterne.

Here at long last our wanderings temporarily ceased. The enemy was no longer pressing on our heels, having probably outstripped his own supply arrangements. Rations galore were piled along the roadside, bully-beef, biscuits, cheese, jam, marmalade, tea, sugar, condensed milk; and we were told to help ourselves. There was no time for paper-work, and if the QM signed for anything, it was only for a fraction of what we took. Such generosity heartened us all.

So we dismounted, put nosebags on the horses, filled our pockets and had a gargantuan breakfast by the roadside. That done, we turned up a lane out of the valley and took up a position just behind a ridge facing east. Here we stood at bay, ready to fight, and somehow feeling that the retreat had gone on long enough.

I went forward and from a small shell-hole (with a signaller-telephonist) registered our six guns on the ridge less than half a mile away. We saw a Boche machine-gunner take up his position on the ridge. A country road ran down the shallow valley between us into the village of Hébuterne. Presently the quiet was broken by the sound of galloping hoofs, as a cart passed between us, driven by an old, white-haired French peasant, standing up in the back and lashing his old horse like a charioteer. I waited for the Boche to kill him, but he didn't fire. A quarter of an hour later, the cart reappeared, the old Frenchman urging his horse up the hill. And what had he rescued from his home in the village at the risk of his life? A large family mattress of course! It was lashed on like a huge sausage roll. *Vive l'amour!* And to hell with the war. I laughed, but as he came abreast the German machine-gunner opened up with bursts of fire, not to kill, just to frighten him. But while the bullets missed the Frenchman, they damn nearly got me. I was flat down in my small shell-hole and fancied I could feel the bullets combing my hair. It was not at all funny! At least not until the old man and his mattress had passed up the hill and the German's bursts of fire were directed at his tail-board. Then we had a good laugh; and because the German had spared the old man's life, we spared him! But that afternoon we wiped out an enemy attack before it even reached our thinly held infantry line. That and similar resistance on our flanks put a final stop to the German advance in our section. He never got further. Our retreat was at an end.

However, what a state we were in! For six days and

nights we had been on the move, in and out of action, and all of us were near the end of our tether. The pale begrimed faces of the men and their lacklustre eyes told a tale of heavy strain, little food, and even less sleep. Most of the horses too were in a poor way, with their heads hanging down and their ribs showing. Some were badly galled, having had their harness on continuously for a week. But we were lucky to have come through with the loss of only eight men and twenty horses, and to be the only battery in the division that had lost none of its guns.

That evening, 26 March, to our great relief, Captain Stanley Jones returned fresh from leave and took command of the battery (I had commanded it during two days and nights of running battle and was just about done!). Many were the congratulations when we saw the crowns on his shoulder-straps and knew that he was confirmed as major commanding A/112 Battery. In smart tunic and beautifully cut riding breeches he went the rounds greeting us all cheer-fully; and the very sight of him did us all a power of good. At nightfall, the major kept only half the gunners on duty by the guns, while the other half took off their boots and uniforms for the first time since the battle began, scooped cubby-holes in the bank of a sunken road, huddled into their blankets and fell into a deep stupor of sleep. Next morning most of us had our first wash and shave for a week – and then it was the turn of the other half of the battery to go off duty.

It amused me to recall how like we were to an earlier English army that once camped overnight not many miles to the north-west of us, near a village called Azincourt.

> The poor condemnéd English,
> Like sacrifices, by their watchful fires
> Sit patiently, and inly ruminate
> The morning's danger; and their gesture sad,

Investing lank-lean cheeks and war worn coats,
Presenteth them unto the gazing moon
So many horrid ghosts. O now, who will behold
The royal captain of this ruined band,
Walking from watch to watch, from tent to tent . . .*
That every wretch, pining and pale before
Beholding him, plucks comfort from his looks . . .
A little touch of Harry in the night.

Our Major Jones had something of that little touch; from which many of us must have plucked comfort.

On the 28th the weather turned very wet, and we were ordered to move a couple of miles to the south. The guns were brought into action in front of a slightly sunken road between Mailly-Maillet and Colincamps. We were quite without material for shelters, until I remembered seeing an engineer's dump near Colincamps, when the leave-train brought me up the line. To this dump I therefore took a wagon with a party of gunners and, working rather hastily because it was under long-range shell-fire, we collected enough timber, corrugated iron and sandbags to make some roadside shelters for the men so that they could be out of the rain. On the following day, we managed to remove an entire wooden hut on our wagon, for use as the Officers' Mess. Thus life became a little more settled and there was time to think of writing another letter home. When I did so, however, it was not yet 'peacetime warfare' that could be recorded.

April 1st. A/112 R.F.A.
I am alive, you may be glad to hear! And have had quite enough war to last me for a bit, since I saw you.

---

* The standard of accommodation in 1415 seems to have been better than in 1918.

You should have seen us when the retreat ended. No one had washed or had boots or clothes off for the past week, and we were all in a most awful state of dirt and unshavenness. The men were smoking the last of the Coronas that the Quartermaster-Sergeant had lifted from the Bapaume canteen before the Boche reached it. But we are all clean now, and living in little cubby-holes scooped in the bank of a sunken road, with the guns out in front.

Yesterday it poured with rain and many of us were soaked to the skin. I have built myself a bedroom in the bank of the road; two feet high, two feet wide and seven feet long, like a coffin with the end knocked off. Not very roomy, but at least it keeps the rain out.

April 5th. A/112 R.F.A.

Last night I was on liaison duty with the infantry at Battalion H.Q. in a nearby village. At 5.30 this morning they made a small attack to improve their position; and almost at once the Boche started a terrific bombardment of the whole of our sector. 5.9s rained into the village, and the cellar that is Battalion H.Q. was rocking and shuddering with the concussion of shells. This went on from 6 a.m. to 9 a.m., at which time I was due to return to the battery. I knew I was needed there. How we got out of that village I don't know. The whole air was thick with shell-fumes, and humming and droning with pieces of shell. However, my telephonist and I just went straight ahead and came through it O.K.

The battery was also getting it in the neck when we reached them, and I noticed a German sausage-balloon that was probably directing fire on us. The gun-crews were not liking it much, as there had not been time to sink the pits properly, and they had only a few sand-bags as protection against the flying splinters. But we had to keep firing in answer to S.O.S. calls; so, to encourage them, Major Jones and I strolled about in the open, he watching the guns on the right, I on the left. I smoked my new pipe and tried to appear unconcerned, though some of the shells burst only a matter of yards away. Fortunately the ground was soft from the rain, and they were sending over percussion H.E., so the bursts were very localised – a good job for us it wasn't shrapnel. From their glances I gathered that some of the chaps thought we were daft. So did I, but I felt furious and didn't care.

One of the bombardiers of my section who was carrying ammunition up to his gun got a direct hit a few paces from me. There was a flash and he just folded up. As I got my arms round him, blood poured from his chest, his eyes turned up, and he was gone. We covered the crumpled bloody heap with a blanket and carried on. Several other men were wounded as well.

By 2 p.m. the Hun attacks had been finally repulsed and things quietened down. My bombardier was a jolly good fellow, and was going to be promoted corporal today. We had also put him in for a Military Medal. Now I shall have to break the news to his people.

There are rumours that we are shortly going north to a quieter spot, and we'll be quite ready to go. However it's another big show safely weathered, and good experience, so I am not sorry. But I do hate being just an Aunt Sally for their guns. After the humiliation of retreat, the worm in me has turned, and I want to get at them! I wish I had been born 200 years ago when, with war cries and the skirl of pipes, the Gordons would have charged the enemy with the claymore. Hot blooded fighting would have come much more easily; like a furious forward charge at rugger, only more so.

April 6th. A/112 Brigade – same spot
Things don't seem to have quietened down yet. Yesterday I went forward to the front line for liaison duty with the New

Zealand Division, which has relieved the tattered remains of our own infantry. What a grand crowd they are! Sunburnt, powerful, steady men – they look as if they had just yesterday come from their cattle or sheep ranches to put things to rights here; and they are completely confident that they can wipe the floor with the Boches, though they talk quietly and without boasting.

The section of trench that I was in had been taken by the Huns during an attack two days before; but some hours later these N.Z. chaps had counter-attacked and thrown them out, taking 200 prisoners and no less than 102 light machine-guns. The trench was still littered with enemy equipment, rifles and ammunition. I even ate a piece of Hun ration bread – very poor stuff. They had been burying Huns overnight, but some still lay about and the whole neighbourhood smelt pretty whiffy.

I went down a sap, squinted over the top, and very soon in an old trench opposite spotted a Boche. He also spotted me. I clearly saw him prop a light machine-gun on the parapet and point it at me. There was just time to duck as a stream of bullets went cracking into the parapet above my head. So I moved back to our O.P., borrowed a periscope, and told my signaller to ring up the battery. Within five minutes I had a shower of H.E. shells bursting on and around his trench. We heard no more from him or his gun. I finished off with some 'bouncing H.E.' – a new idea of ours – and the air-bursts looked pretty effective.*

A short time afterwards, things became extraordinarily warm from their shell-fire, and it looked as if an attack was coming. We all sat tight at the bottom of the trench, but several of the infantry were knocked out. I rang up the

---

* This involved firing shells with a delayed fuse on a shallow trajectory, so that they bounced off the ground and burst above the enemy lines.

battery and asked them to stand by; and also got a rifle and ammunition from a chap who was beyond using it.

After about an hour of this, when everyone was about fed up with the shelling, the barrage lifted, and Huns could be seen emerging from their trenches and advancing towards us. This was what the N.Z. boys had hoped for. My line to the battery being by a miracle still intact, I sent through the S.O.S. call. Within seconds our shells were bursting over them and thinning them out. As they came nearer, I leaned over the parapet and opened up with my rifle, along with the rest who were firing steadily. It was a thrilling, mad, desperate moment. I certainly got one of them, a great big chap, and possibly others, but was too excited to notice how many. The whole ground in front of us was covered in dead Boches. The attack broke about 50 yards from our trench, the few who reached it were bayonetted or knocked over the head, and the remainder broke and ran for it. I hoped we would go after them, but these New Zealanders knew better, and sat tight. Matters thus ended quite satisfactorily for us, and there was no more trouble during my spell of duty.

Coming back to the battery, I passed through an old communication trench so chock full of dead Huns that I had to tread on their bodies. They had been killed by bombs and were in a shocking state, sprawling and distorted. Altogether I've had enough of it for the time being, and am glad to hear we are shortly to move.

P.S. *April 8th*. We moved out at 1 a.m. this morning in buckets of rain. Had an awful job to get the guns out of the pits.

April 9th (evening). A/112 Bde. R.F.A. On the road
I'm not sure how long we shall take to get to our destination, so this will be a running letter. We are bound for a very quiet spot about fifty miles to the north, just west of a

town whose name resembles an army weeping.* There's no denying we badly need a rest. The horses are in such a state that we can't do more than about ten miles a day. We have to be continually padding the harness and tying up fresh galls, and there is a long string of animals unfit for draught work that forms the tail of the battery. We have had to make mixed teams of horses and mules to draw the guns and wagons, and many of them are four-horse teams only. Gun-shields are dented and marked, and plenty of wheel-spokes splintered or chipped by machine-gun bullets. Some of the men are queer sights too, some wearing sou'westers and even cloth caps, and gum-boots or waders instead of boots, and all are in a ragged condition.

My own trench-boots gave out three days ago. The stitching at both heels and one toe parted, and the soles simply disappeared in the mud; so I've been walking about on the welt with holes in it. During the past rainy week I've never had dry feet, though one gets used to that. Yesterday however I was able to buy a pair of boots and puttees from a French shop, and I've thrown my old ones away. I also bought handkerchiefs, socks and a change of underclothing; so my luggage now comprises a sandbag as well as the ruck-sack! The Q.M. got me a tin-hat, gas-bag and blanket some days ago – so I'm doing quite well. Field glasses and revolver I may get later, but I don't need them at present.

I missed Harris' services during the fighting. Owing to casualties we put the batmen back on battery duties, but now that we are out of the line he's taking me in hand again, and tonight is to be laundry night!

This afternoon I went ahead to look at our billets, and on the way back thought it would be nice to take Fly off the road and let her stretch her legs across country. She thought so too, now that her sugar ration has been restored. After a

* Armentières.

good canter we came on a small farm-house and, thinking I
might be able to buy a couple of bottles of local wine, I tied
her up and knocked at the door.

An old man opened it and his wife welcomed me in. It
was evident that they were very poor; and when I made my
carefully rehearsed inquiry, 'Est-ce-que je peux acheter du
vin, s'il vous plait?' there was much wringing of hands. But
they produced a chipped tea cup and a half-empty bottle of
greenish liquid and pressed me to drink it.

We conversed, subject to my limited vocabulary, and
they showed me two photographs of their uniformed sons,
elaborately framed in front of a little crucifix on a side-
table. But when I asked where they were, they just said
'Morts, tous les deux'. I mumbled 'Je suis si triste' (the
nearest I could get to 'I'm so sorry'). Then the old woman
took my hand, and stood pathetically holding it in hers; till
I broke the tension by suddenly saying 'Vive la France!' –
and drained the contents of the tea-cup. (It tasted frightful!)
Smiling through her tears, she replied 'Vive les Ecossais!'
Then I gave the old man my cigarettes and rode off amid
mutual cries of 'Bonne chance!' Poor souls, I hope life will
be kinder to them some day.

(11th April)
We were greatly looking forward to reaching our rest-home
tomorrow; but now we hear the balloon's gone up and we
are walking straight into another battle! The Hun has taken
Armentières and is pushing westwards, and the gunfire
seems to be getting louder. No more now. I'll try to post this
tomorrow, when I know more of what's happening.

(12th April)
We are approaching the battle area over the shoulder of
Mont des Cats, and have halted for a few minutes to give
the horses a breather after climbing the hill. It is a

beautifully clear afternoon, and eastwards all across the Flanders Plain I can see clouds of smoke arising from burning dumps, etc. The guns are hard at it, so before long we'll be in action again. So much for our longed-for rest. I hope to get this off right away. Meanwhile don't worry.

We came down off the hill, moved into a field at St Jans Cappel, half a mile north-west of Bailleul, parked guns and wagons, unharnessed the horses, and prepared to spend the night there. Refugees were pouring out of the town, some riding with their belongings stacked high on farm carts, other humbler folk with their household goods precariously balanced on wheelbarrows, which they surely could not hope to take very far.

Just as I was wondering whether there would be time for a last-minute raid on the Bailleul Officers' Club, where I had once dined so lavishly in the presence of General Plumer, orders reached us to clear out quickly: the Germans had entered the town in strength, and might emerge from it at any moment. Our move was conducted with quite exemplary speed; and within an hour we came into action about three miles from Bailleul on the lower slopes of Mont des Cats, a hill which rises steeply with Mount Kemmel and others to some 400 feet above the Flanders plain and was likely to be the enemy's main local objective.

Here we were greatly impeded by the occupants of the adjoining farm, which we were hoping to occupy. They refused to leave, and denied us access to any of the farm buildings – even the barns and horse-troughs. But a few ranging shots from our guns in the direction of the enemy persuaded them that danger was too near; and before long they left. As they moved out, our QMS moved in, and that night the mess cooks gave us chicken for supper!

Next morning, we moved forward down the hill, and came

into action near a farm on the lower slopes, about a mile north-west of the village of Meteren.

Later a document arrived by runner. Major Jones read it, and handed it round to the officers without comment. It read as follows:

To all ranks of the British Forces in France.

Three weeks ago today the enemy began his terrific attacks against us on a 50-mile front. His objects are to separate us from the French, to take the Channel ports, and destroy the British Army.

In spite of throwing already 106 Divisions into the battle and enduring the most reckless sacrifice of human life, he has as yet made little progress towards his goal.

We owe this to the determined fighting and self-sacrifice of our troops. Words fail me to express the admiration which I feel for the splendid resistance offered by all ranks of our Army under the most trying circumstances.

Many amongst us now are tired. To those I would say that Victory will belong to the side which holds out the longest. The French Army is moving rapidly and in great force to our support . . .

There is no other course open to us but to fight it out! Every position must be held to the last man: there must be no retirement. With our backs to the wall, and believing in the justice of our cause, each one of us must fight on to the end. The safety of our Homes and the Freedom of Mankind alike depend upon the conduct of each one of us at this critical moment.

Thursday, 11th April, 1918

D. Haig.
F.M.

I got the general idea; but somehow this modern version of the 'little touch of Harry in the night' did not inspire me; in fact the rhetoric made me critical. There was not the remotest contact between us and the Olympian figures at GHQ; there never had been. How did he know how A/112 were placed? It was almost two days since this circular was signed and a good many walls had already been given up during that time. Against which particular walls must our backs now be placed? And this talk of our fighting 'to the end' sounded as if we were somehow cornered and the game was up. Surely it was the Boche, not us, who would some day find himself in that situation! Uneasily, I handed it back without comment. Little else was said. Resignedly we prepared for a fight to the finish.

Throughout that day we combined occasional bursts of harassing fire at the enemy with the process of making ourselves comfortable. We did not waste time in digging gun-pits as the guns were well hidden behind a straggling hedge; but we prepared large ammunition recesses alongside each gun, and stocked them to capacity. The guns were oiled and cleaned and carefully checked over.

I had got my Centre Section gunners into a barn; and when I paid them a last visit they were romping about in the hay, and ready for anything that the morning might bring. As Sergeant Durney said, all they wanted now was for the Boche to advance up the hill, and for our ammunition supply to be kept going. And his blue eyes gleamed as he smiled with grim anticipation.

Just before we turned in, a machine-gun officer arrived in great distress. He had established six machine-gun posts in front of Meteren village. But the Boche had brought a field-gun up to a farm near their front line, and had spotted and destroyed every single one of his posts. The poor chap broke down as he told us this; so Major Jones filled him up with whisky, gave him a shake-down for the night, and promised to deal with it in the morning.

Next day, Sunday, 14th April, Major Jones took me and a couple of signallers forward to deal with that gun. On the way we called in at a company HQ in a farm just behind Meteren. The infantry were there, deepening a ditch along a hedgerow to form a trench. The company commander told us that the village was effectively in no-man's-land. He, our major and myself walked into the kitchen garden to discuss how best to get at this gun. We must have been under direct observation, because a Hun sniper opened up on us. I would have liked to take cover, which seems sensible when someone is aiming at you; but the company commander probably wanted to impress his men, and as he wouldn't take cover, neither would Major Jones. The position was ridiculous. The Hun fired and fired, and missed and missed, while we stood on the path remarking on the excellence of the cabbages, each inwardly vowing that he would not be the one to suggest a move! Eventually however, honour was satisfied, and Major Jones and I left our signallers under cover, and went forward to find an O.P. in the village.

On a rise at the north end of Meteren stood an old wooden windmill, which seemed ideal except that the staircase was on the side facing the enemy. We raced up the steps hoping not to be noticed; and were relieved that no one fired at us. Major Jones went to the window with his field-glasses to see what could be seen, and while he was thus occupied I took a look round the mill. I had never been in a windmill before. It had a warm, floury smell, and I was fascinated by the ingenious machinery, huge wheels and cogs of solid wood with a beautiful grain and pattern, polished by the friction of years to a perfect glaze. There was not a drop of oil on it and I longed to see it working. Major Jones was less pleased. He had found that some tree-branches interfered with our view of the farm. I too was trying to see our target when a shrapnel shell burst in the air a few feet past the window. 'They've seen us,' he said, and we went down the stairs even faster than we had come up.

As we hurried forward into the village, a shell crashed into the house opposite, bringing bricks, tiles and plaster down in a shower over us, and we wondered who was stalking who! We separated to search independently, and I entered a small villa, hoping for a view from a bedroom window. In the hall I found two sheep tethered to a cast-iron hat-stand. It must have been an unusual experience for them and they were baa-ing in terror. I cut them loose and they bolted out of the door to freedom. 'Good luck,' I called, 'and keep going!' There was no doubt they understood. Climbing the stairs, I found that the front of the bedroom had been blown away and we would have no cover there. Major Jones also had had no luck. 'We want to get nearer,' he said.

By now we had reached the front of the village, where there were no buildings to hide us. We could see that, if we crossed a garden and got into the small field beyond it, we would have a clear view of the Boche gun and, in fact, be within a few hundred yards of it. But there was little cover and we would have to move quickly. 'Come on,' said Major Jones, and together we dashed across the garden. Almost at once a machine gun opened up on us. The hedge, through which we hoped to burst into the field beyond, turned out to have a barbed-wire fence on our side of it. But we mounted the wire, jumped over the hedge and, rushing across that small field, flung ourselves into a ditch.

Machine-gun bullets were sweeping the field. They seemed to be coming from inside an abandoned YMCA marquee a few hundred yards away. But the view from the roots of the hedge was good. We could see the muzzle and shield of a field-gun, framed in the arched entrance of the farm building, and some grey figures beside it. So far, so good; all we needed now was a telephone line to our battery.

I looked back across the field. The end nearest to the village was bounded by a brick wall with a green door. But the shortest way was the way by which we had come. I waited a couple of minutes until the machine-gunner, having no target, stopped firing.

'I shan't be long,' I said, slipping off my haversack and gas-mask, tin hat and revolver.

'All right,' replied the Major, 'I'll keep an eye on them. Good luck!'

Creeping out of the ditch I raced, head down, for the hedge. It was a thorn hedge and a thick one at that. As I reached for the barbed wire beyond, the machine gun opened up again. Bullets that whine and hiss are meant for someone else, but these were making loud cracks – near misses. I got one hand across to the wire, but as often as I pushed forward, the hedge thrust me back. No good. I dropped flat on my face, while burst after burst from the machine-gun sliced the air overhead.

The only chance now was the green door in the brick wall, some thirty yards further on. Waiting for a lull in the firing, I jumped up and ran for it. Bullets cracked past. I seized the door handle, turned it both ways and shook the door. Locked! I turned away and – CRASH!

Half-blinded by brick-dust and shell-fumes, my head ringing and with a stabbing pain in my chest, I struggled to reach the ditch at the end of the wall. There, when collapse came, I would be below the bullets and off the line of fire of a second shell. Then I went down, and coughed, and tasted the salt blood in my throat. Mustn't cough any more, then. I lay still, staring at a bunch of nettles, and wondering why they didn't sting my hand that was in their midst.

Presently, I felt hands on me. It was Major Jones kneeling at my back. 'Get down,' I said, for the bullets were still sweeping the field. The hands were now tying something round my thigh. Then –

'Have the blighters got me at last?'

'No, you'll be all right!'

He tried to make it sound convincing but I guessed how things were.* The firing eased up; no more shells, no more bullets. I felt very tired and drifted away ... The rattle of machine-gun fire brought me back to consciousness – burst after burst, menacing, relentless. Presently it stopped, and there were voices.

'Have you got him? Right, lift.'

Gentle hands lifted me sideways on to a stretcher.

I tried to protest – several stretcher-bearers and Major Jones – not to mention me: what a target! We wouldn't stand a chance. What was the use anyway?

But they didn't seem to hear.

'Are you ready? Up!'

The stretcher came up shoulder-high.

'Off we go then!'

This was madness – I shrank into myself, waiting for the bullets to rip into us.

Nothing happened.

Slowly the stretcher was taken through the wrecked doorway; round the corner of a house; and by further stages away and beyond the reach of machine gun or shells ...

And in that day's casualty return, one more gunner subaltern was crossed off the active list.

April 16th, 1918. *Casualty Clearing Station*

As you will see, after ten months of it I have copped out at last! Though I am still a little groggy, I will try to tell you what happened.

I woke up in this Casualty Clearing Station, where my

---

* He told me later he thought I might not last for more than half an hour, so determined to get me away at once.

wounds have been bound up. One through my back and left lung, one in each buttock, one through my left thigh, and a handful of smaller bits in my back and shoulders. I was given 'resuscitation' for a day and night in a very warm ward where they made me drink champagne, port or beer. But I managed to get enough soda water to quench my thirst; and really feel a lot better now. My only trouble is the discomfort of my buttock wounds, as I have to sit up in bed, and my shortness of breath because the pain in my chest prevents me coughing. In a day or two they hope to take the bits out of me, when I reach the Base. Meanwhile, don't worry.

Love from Huntly

P.S. Last night a Frenchman in the bed opposite was in delirium and kept on singing the Marseillaise. At last he shut up, and after a while they carried him out on a stretcher with a Union Jack over it. I shan't try to sing!

At the Base Hospital, Boulogne, things went wrong. They couldn't locate two pieces of the assorted ironmongery. All the wounds turned septic, and my time was evenly divided between the X-ray room, the operating theatre and my bed. Oxygen, brandy and the rest of it. But somehow I came through.

It was then that I received the following letter from Stanley Jones. Its laconic understatement was so typical of him that somehow I felt he was standing by my bedside, giving me the latest news from the battery. And what news it was!

April 24th, 1918. A/112 R.F.A.

Dear Gordon,

I was immensely relieved to get your letter, as I had doubts whether you would pull round. I knew it would be all right if you got to hospital quickly, which you have – so that is all right.

Yes, that was a hell of a day, when Stubbins and Durney went on. We had 27 casualties in men, and 32 in horses, including Fly and my mare, both of whom are remaining at duty. My second charger was killed outright, and all E-sub's gun-team.

Your Centre-Section gunners were all wiped out with one shell.

[*After I took this in, I found I could read no more for a while.*]

I don't know whether you noticed it as you were carried through, but I had to burst that damned door open when I went for the stretcher, and the M.G.'s were flying everywhere. Do you know that the Boche absolutely let us off when we took you back? When I went first, and when I came back with the party, he M.G.-ed us like blazes; but as soon as we appeared with you, he stopped. When I went back with the wire, he started again, so it was no coincidence.

I strafed the farm. I don't know about the gun, but it didn't operate afterwards. We tried to take the village back that night, but N.B.G.

Sgts. Dale, Jinks, Taylor and Signaller Brown got the M.M.

Well, no more news. Let's know how things are with you.'

There are but three things more to add.

The Military Cross was awarded to Major Stanley O. Jones 'for outstanding coolness and courage in superintending the removal of the wounded, and in keeping his battery in action'. To his coolness and courage I owe my life.

Secondly, the Boche never reached our battery position. On those hill slopes he found he was getting more than he could take. A few months later, Sir Douglas Haig launched the series of successful battles that brought total defeat to Germany's armed forces. To quote Sir Winston Churchill:

> From the general not less than from the British point of view, 12th April 1918 was probably, after the Marne, the climax of the war ... Neuve Eglise was lost, and Bailleul and Meteren; and under the intense pressure the front bent backwards. But it did not break. When, on the 17th, eight German divisions, seven of them fresh, were violently repulsed in their attack on the famous hill of Kemmel, the crisis of the Battle of Lys was over. The orders of the Commander had been strictly and faithfully fulfilled.*

Finally, I raise my tin-hat to that unknown German machine-gunner, a true sportsman, without whose forbearance this book could never have been written.

* *The World Crisis 1914–18* by Winston S. Churchill.

Postscript

... and that was where the book, as published in 1967, ended. The story, of course, did not end there. In *Canton More Far*, his unpublished book about his time in China in the 1920s, my father described the aftermath in some detail. From this, and from his meticulous notes and family archive, I have compiled the postscript. So what *did* happen next?

A first description of the news of his injury comes from his younger sister Helena – at the time aged sixteen, living at home and helping to look after her elderly father, who had suffered a series of strokes.

I was at Drumearn [the family home at North Berwick], facing my paralysed father on the sofa, my mother behind him. The maid came in with a telegram, and I had to show no alarm. With great presence of mind my mother quietly said: 'This is to say that Huntly has been wounded and we must be thankful that he is out of the firing line.' Actually, it said: 'Seriously ill, gun-shot wound in chest. Visit impossible.' Because every possible ship was carrying reinforcements for the retreat.

Then a day or two later: 'Dangerously ill. Come at once' and with help from friends, Mother was off. It happened in the Easter holidays and there was I, aged sixteen, having to run a large house in war-time conditions, with a helpless father, a nurse-companion whom we did not much like, and no word for days about my mother or brother. I lost 7 lbs in ten days!

Their mother's memoir continues the story:

With only a few hours to arrange everything, I was off by night train to London, facing the possibility of the death either of my helpless husband from shock, or my sorely wounded son, or perhaps both. It was an agonising position.

I reached the Red Cross hospital and probably helped to bring Huntly back to life, as I was told the staff had hardly been able to keep him going during the night. He had been shot through the back and one lung with fragments of a bursting shell, and only his young and strong physique and the goodness of God brought him through that terrible experience, and the three months of septicaemia that followed. I was allowed to stay in Boulogne for a fortnight, but had to leave him in an unconscious condition after an operation to try and discover the cause of his great pain and abscess.

My father's letters from June 1917 onwards were carefully kept and numbered by his mother, but after 19 April 1918 they cease for a while. The recipient was now sitting beside him; and in any case he was beyond writing. A later note in his hand explains:

A note as to what happened in the hospital in Boulogne: Letter 63 was dated 19th April; I didn't feel too bad, and reported my condition home. But evidently the doctors knew better, and Mother was on her way in response to a War Office message – 'dangerously ill, come at once'.

Three pieces of shell were still in me, of the fourteen bits that had hit me, and every wound had gone septic. It was thought the Germans had poisoned the inner lining of their shells, though this may be doubted. Anyhow I was in for septicaemia, a condition in which pus circulates in the blood-stream, starting fresh abscesses wherever possible – recovery rate, I believe, 10 per cent. Also one piece had smashed a rib, nicked my left lung, emerged again from the rib-cage and hidden itself outside in my left arm-pit, where no one thought of X-raying. It was only the size of a date-stone. Lung wounds then had a recovery rate of 10 per cent. So in those non-penicillin days, I was apparently on a 1 per cent chance.

During the ensuing month, I had five chest operations, several under local anaesthetic, as they didn't like to risk chloroform on only one working lung. The only one which I remember clearly went on for one and a half hours, during which time a very pretty nurse held my hand at intervals. There were trying moments when they cut off the broken ends of my smashed rib, and also cut two inches out of the rib below it to gain better access to the lung cavity which by now was producing a tumblerful of pus twice daily – rather like a cow! After one and a half hours the surgeon asked if I had had enough. In reply I asked him how long he wanted to go on for. He said he didn't know, as they couldn't find anything. I (fortunately) suggested we should call it a day and he readily agreed. There was nothing there.

I remember on another occasion before the ward had been woken up, lying awake and listening to a tap slowly dripping. Presently a nurse appeared, drew back the curtains, and caught sight of something under my bed which appeared to give her a shock. She ran out and returned quickly with two men and a stretcher, and a surgeon – and in about three minutes I was once more in the operating theatre. It appears I had been bleeding for a considerable time – enough to soak through the mattress and make a sizeable pool on the floor.

They stopped the bleeding, and in due course I was returned to bed – on a new mattress! But I must have been drained unpleasantly low. In those days there were no blood-banks, so the main thing was to fill up my veins with something. A saline fluid of similar consistency to blood, but without any of those helpful little cells, was the best available. They opened a vein on my right ankle, shoved in a tube and I watched the fluid trickle out of a glass jar, which when empty was replaced by another one. Meanwhile, I was given a mask through which to breathe oxygen from a cylinder, bubbled through brandy, which was reviving as well as pleasant. Another nasty corner turned.

At last the piece that nearly did me in was located in my left arm-pit. It had been there a month, situated inside a complex jumble of arteries, veins and nerves that supply the arm, where it had produced a large abscess. I was very lucky it had got there without cutting any of those vessels, etc. The surgeon, having opened up the surface flesh above and below the arm-joint, did the whole operation of extracting the piece with his bare fingers, both hands at once, as he wouldn't risk using cutting instruments. The nurses said he really did a wonderful job. Anyhow, the piece was later presented to me in a little parcel of lint in a tin box; and Mother had it mounted as a brooch!

Mothers were normally only allowed a visit of one week to wounded men on the critical list; but they let her stay nearly three weeks – and she greatly helped my recovery. After she had gone home, I wrote Letter 64, dated 8th May.

As the handwriting shows – and the inaccuracy over dates
also – I wasn't too good at that time. Subsequent letters were
written by the chaplain, till they got all the pieces out; and
then by the end of May things were getting a bit more
normal and I was able to write again.

Though the initial crisis was over, his condition
improved only slowly. Wounded in mid-April, it was late
June before he tried to stand up for the first time; July
before he took a first few triumphant steps across the ward.
Meanwhile, tubes were inserted to drain the wound every
two hours, and Dakin's Fluid disinfectant pumped in (and
out) of his chest cavity. At one point they even turned him
over and filled the cavity up from a measure; to what end is
unclear, but apparently he held thirteen fluid ounces –
nearly a pint!

Although London was almost as far from his Scottish
home as Boulogne, he longed to cross the Channel. In late
June he wrote, 'I feel if I could only get over to Blighty I
would heal ever so much more easily than I am doing here.'
But the doctors would not move him while his temperature
hovered stubbornly between 99° and 100°F, as his body
fought the infection within. In desperation, he tried to speed
things up by sucking air into the side of his mouth to cool
the thermometer; but rather overdid it, so that his cheery
enquiry of 'How is it today, Nurse?' was met with
'Well, according to this you must be dead: now put it in
properly!'

At last, in mid-July, the chest wounds miraculously
ejected two fragments of rib smashed by the shell, and the
discharge began to lessen; later that month, by far
the longest inhabitant on the ward, he was deemed fit
enough to be moved. In an early draft of *Canton More Far*
he recorded the day he had so longed for:

I was among a batch of wounded being brought back from Boulogne to London. After a glassy-smooth Channel crossing the train carried us slowly and gently through the Kentish orchards, and at nightfall drew in to Charing Cross station. There the stretchers were laid out in rows on the platform and we lay staring up into the dirty, friendly roof. We, who had almost given up hope of survival, were home at last. It was a hot night, I remember, and they left the ambulance door open. Outside on the pavement of the Strand, in spite of the lateness of the hour, a little crowd of women waited patiently. As our ambulance emerged from the station courtyard, they raised a cheer and threw in a handful of roses. Nothing could have been more touching than this welcome from total strangers. 'Roses! For Christ's sake!' exclaimed the stretcher above me; and he spoke for us all.

Presently the ambulance stopped at 16 Bruton Street, Lady Evelyn Mason's Nursing Home, and I was carried into the darkened ward and lifted into bed. When the doctor had looked me over, a young nurse gave me some barley-water to drink, and helped me to get comfortable on the pillows. At my request she pulled up the blind a little so that I could see out into the street. (I could also see that she was very lovely, and quite unlike those bustling middle-aged nurses in the Base hospital.) Far too excited to sleep, I lay there and gazed at the street lamps and the houses opposite, and tried to believe that everything I saw was real and not just a dream. Presently men started hosing the roadway to make it clean and fresh for the morning. The swishing sound of the water seemed to be gradually washing away something of the filth and horror of the year gone by. I was weak and tired; and the thought of those friends who would never again come home blurred my eyes with tears.

I did not see her cross the ward, but suddenly a hand touched my shoulder and a voice whispered, 'Forget about it. It's all over now.' A kiss brushed my cheek, and she was gone. Next morning, she gave me a smile as she went off duty – a private little smile – and that was the last I saw of her.

Later I heard she had to go to her mother who had been taken ill. All I could find out was her name – Prudence Amery.

At Lady Evelyn's his recovery began in earnest. On most days he was pushed in a wheelchair along Bruton Street and into Berkeley Square, to sit in the shade of the old summer-house. A kind person sent tickets to a variety show at the Coliseum, where he found the turns moved him either to hysterical laughter or silent weeping. 'Now that it was possible to relax, my feelings were quite out of control. It was embarrassing beyond words.' Grock the Clown in particular was so brilliantly funny that he had to spin around and look away, suddenly aware that his bandaged chest was about to burst, this time with laughter!

From *Canton More Far* again:

With recovery in sight, my mind began to turn to the future, a shadowy period of unknown length and prospects, which ever since the day that shell burst on the Meteren door-post had remained quite unexplored. When asked what the future held for me, the senior surgeon on the Medical Board was frank in his reply. 'Your Army career is over,' he said, 'though as a Regular you'll get a small pension for life. You will have to take things very slowly at first, and always avoid anything exciting or energetic. Muffle up in cold weather, or that lung may flare up again. Remember you are permanently disabled. But don't be too depressed. You may have quite a few years of life yet. They do say it's the cracked pitcher that goes longest to the well.'

That seemed to me a fair summing up, and one that should be put to the test in due course. But two phrases stood out. A pension for life; a piece of unbelievable generosity, though the actual money did not amount to much. And no more work; a grateful nation looking after my every need, and my immediate friends tirelessly attentive to my comfort.

As the time approached for me to leave the London Nursing Home, I applied for a transfer to North Berwick, for it seemed that one might best settle down to a lotus-eating existence in one's own home. That was a mistake. Not only were the family not in sympathy with lotus-eating, but in the bracing climate of the Firth of Forth, it lost its attraction for me also. The golf course that had seemed beyond my hopes beckoned again, and soon a putter replaced the walking stick in my hand. Each day marked some further advance on the Western Front and some further stage in my own recovery. At last repeated Allied victories in the field brought the war to an end on 11th November, at about the same time as I managed to complete my first round of the nine-hole children's course.*

Next I determined to become more mobile. But a car could not be hired, nor was petrol obtainable. To this challenge there was no easy answer. Eventually, I found an undertaker who had an old motor-hearse and a petrol allowance. So at times when this cumbersome vehicle was not officially in use, it could be seen navigating the less-frequented country roads with the owner and myself alternately at the wheel. Almost invariably other users of the road gave us a wide berth – not surprising, in view of our

---

* Ten days later, he and the other injured officers at Carl Kemp Nursing Home witnessed the gratifying spectacle of the entire German fleet – 370 ships – sail up the Firth of Forth in surrender. It really was over.

massive display of plate glass and brass knobs, and the sudden thought that any day we might be taking them for their last ride.

In this and other ways I set out to test whether the gloomy forecast of my physical limitations could not somehow be overcome; for it was obvious that on this would depend whether I really had to accept the handicaps of a semi-invalid, or whether a little boldness might not win back for me the priceless gift of robust health for the rest of my life.

These hopes and dreams came to a head one autumn morning when, without waking the household, I left in the half-dark on a bicycle with a small basket and three stale ginger biscuits, and made my way eastwards from North Berwick up on to the high golf links towards Canty Bay. There near the cliff-edge I sat down and gazed out over the calm silver expanse to watch the sun rise out of the North Sea. It was the experience of a lifetime. The deserted links, the crystal cold air, the awe-inspiring silence gradually broken by the overhead twittering of unseen skylarks; and then the breathtaking moment when the sun imperceptibly broke the horizon and slowly rose in all its majesty to start a new day.

I looked around and, finding myself still quite alone, felt suddenly compelled to kneel down and pray. Firstly in silent awareness of the glory around me; then in profound thankfulness for my survival; then to be given energy and strength for full recovery, that instead of being a burden to others I might some day be of use to them, and repay something of what I had received. It was a silent prayer, but came from the depths of my being. Then I filled the little basket with mushrooms, ate my soft ginger biscuits, and with a last look at the sea, now in full golden sunlight, turned and slowly cycled home. My mother must have noticed that my outlook had changed; my intention was now in every way to be up and doing; but tactfully and approvingly, she said nothing.

But up and doing what? My brother was shortly due to come home for a few days from London, where he was going into private practice. He and my medical-minded mother were the only surviving relatives or close friends to whom I could look for advice. It was hardly surprising therefore that the upshot of our discussion was that I should study medicine, as I had already had a good foretaste of the wards.

So in the spring of 1919 I took over my brother's bed-sitter in Finchley, a room with a pleasant outlook over some tennis courts and trees in a square. Bart's Medical School was part of London University, and so I had first to take the London Matriculation Exam, though I reckoned that my entry exam for Woolwich, taken three years before, would act as a safety net. And I needed it. A few weeks at a 'crammer' showed that much of what I had learned had been driven out by recent unforgettable experiences; and that some of the things I once knew for certain, I could now only guess at. On the third afternoon of the exam things came to a head, and I could only hand in a blank sheet, on which was written –'Sorry, unwell.'

The result was unexpected.

A few days later, as requested, I reported to the Dean of Bart's, a friendly, frock-coated old man with a beard and twinkly eyes. I was in uniform, blue-banded.* He enquired after my health, and I assured him it was improving steadily. Then he came round from behind his desk and, putting his arm round my shoulders, said quietly, 'Don't worry. You're in.'

As things turned out, my father did not stick with medicine. Corralled with young students from a new generation that had missed the war, he was oppressed both

*A blue band indicated 'wounded'.

by the mortality rate in those pre-antibiotic days and by the lack of income, with the consequent restriction of his social life.

After three years, a chance encounter with an old school friend led to a job with Shell Oil. The salary was an encouraging £600 a year; but they promptly sent him to China, and a Maugham-esque three years in Hong Kong, Canton and beyond – 'more far', as the locals called it – followed (an unhappy adventure which I shall not even attempt to summarise here). After an eventful three years he returned to find Britain in the throes of the 1926 General Strike. With public service still in mind, and little else on offer, he joined London Transport and began a long career with them, starting as a bus inspector. This led to one last, rather extraordinary tale, which he related some years later:

In 1928, as a newly promoted Chief Depot Inspector, I had to interview a certain Driver Brown, who had been late twice in a week in taking out his early-turn bus. As his only reason was that he had overslept, I read him a short lecture on the need for punctuality in a public service, cautioned him and asked him to sign his record. Smiling slightly, he signed.

Then, as he turned to go, he stopped. ''scuse me, sir, could I have a word with you? Was you by any chance the young lootenant that was wounded in front of Meteren?' Very surprised, I admitted that I was – 'But how on earth do you know that?'

'Well, sir,' he replied simply, 'I was your signaller that helped carry you in. I'm very glad to see you came through all right.'

My mind flicked back to 1918 and groped among the remains of an experience that I had been well content to leave buried and forgotten. This was Signaller Brown, who had been with me, and had won the Military Medal for his part in salvaging me, in full view of the Boche machine gun at close range.

I took him by the hand. 'You helped save my life – and now look what the hell I've done – put a caution on your clean record!' And I took out my pen-knife to scratch out the entry. 'No, sir, I was late and you must let it stand,' he insisted. 'Well, that's the last caution you'll get from me,' I laughed; and with that we went round to a nearby hostelry. I sent him three bottles of whisky every Christmas, until he left the Company a few years later, and we lost touch.

Afterword

Where does a story end? As the Postscript may suggest, every time I dipped into the old chest that held my father's papers, I found more that could be added. But there, for now at least, we must leave him, forging a life and building a family in the inter-war years of the twentieth century.

Even though I knew a lot about his life, delving into the archive was an extraordinary voyage. I found unknown drafts, short stories and letters. A string-tied parcel held his letters from the War, and history seemed to burst from them as I unwrapped the pile. On top was a small, white envelope: the actual letter from his friend Geoffrey Robinson in 1915 ('Well, Cheer-oh and good luck' . . .) that was still in his pocket when Robinson's name was posted on the chapel door, killed at the battle of Loos. A much later correspondence revealed that Viscount Montgomery of Alamein was, after Siegfried Sassoon, his first choice for a Foreword. (Sassoon sent his best wishes, but was terminally ill when approached.) As a young officer, Montgomery had been wounded in Meteren in 1914, but despite the connection – and perhaps mercifully – he declined. After publication, other letters from old soldiers uncovered shared emotions, and gratitude for putting into print what so many had felt, but never expressed. 'Oh, the pity of it', as one summarised Passchendaele.

The papers also reveal how my father, like so many others, struggled with life and purpose for some time after that experience. In 1926 he refers to 'post-war restlessness', and records grisly nightmares in which 'I would drag myself through the morasses of no-man's-land . . . invariably I was typecast as the complete coward!' In later correspondence he challenged the trendy revisionism of the 1960s, when the war was simplistically damned as a jingoistic adventure, and 'Lions led by Donkeys', which must have so hurt those who were neither. As this book shows, the reality was infinitely more subtle. Can anyone make complete sense of the Great War? The dichotomy is summed up by the poem he had originally chosen to preface the book:

Back
They ask me where I've been,
And what I've done and seen.
But what can I reply
Who know it wasn't I,
But someone just like me,
Who went across the sea
And with my head and hands,
Killed men in foreign lands . . .
Though I must bear the blame,
Because he bore my name.

In the end he chose Sassoon's poem; only this year did I fully realise the significance of the line that gives the book its name. Even those who came back had lost something irretrievable, and were 'not youth any longer'. The poem also bears a message to his men, lying now in the military cemetery at Meteren. Earlier this year, on the 95th anniversary of their deaths, my own military stiff upper lip came in useful, as a bugler played the Last Post over the 800-odd graves, and after a due silence I read out:

> 'O my brave brown companions, when your souls
>   flock silently away . . .'

There is another, related theme that I detected in all this. Many friends have recalled old relatives who were in the First World War, and how they 'never talked about it'. But from his first letters home, my father seems to have treated writing as his confessional, his outlet for things that could not be expressed in public. Letters were written in impossible conditions, and at improbable hours of the day or night. 'Forgive this outpouring. It's good to get it off one's chest . . . it will be easier now to keep up the pretence that it's all quite good fun out here, with nothing to worry about but the mud.'

It worked: it was an achievement to come out of that War with one's sanity intact. If the 'talking cure' needs a testimonial, you hold it in your hands! Above all, he was determined to hold on to his humanity, in some of the most inhuman circumstances that mankind has ever devised for itself.

And for those of us privileged to have known him, there can be no doubt at all that he succeeded. He was a dear man and a kind father, loving and loved. To our great good fortune, he lived well into old age. In later years, he once again took to wearing his old 'British Warm' officer's greatcoat. On the back of it, the observant eye might detect a scattering of holes, neatly mended: his quiet defiance of Boche, of shrapnel, of Medical Officers, and – into his 85th year – of Time itself.

David Gordon
Allowenshay, Somerset
August 2013

Photo Acknowledgements

All photos come from the author's collection except where otherwise acknowledged. Every effort has been made to trace copyright holders, but any who have been overlooked are invited to get in touch with the publishers.

Page 5 bottom: Imperial War Museum/Q 6236; page 6 top: National Library of Scotland; page 7 bottom: Imperial War Museum/Q 8596; page 8 top: Imperial War Museum 8572.

Huntly Strathearn Gordon was born in Perthshire in 1898. Educated at Clifton College, he joined the Royal Field Artillery in 1916. By June 1917 he was on the Western Front. He survived the war and studied medicine, but having 'seen too many people die' he gave up his studies in 1923 and went to work for Shell Oil in China. Three years later he returned to the UK, where he joined London Transport, rising to be Chief Welfare Officer. During the Blitz, he initiated food trains for the thousands of refugees sheltering in the Underground, and was awarded an MBE. Much of his spare time was spent working with Sir Mortimer Wheeler, using his artillery training to survey archaeological sites in England and France. He married twice, and had four children. *The Unreturning Army* was first published in 1967 and a second book, *The Minister's Wife*, in 1978. Huntly Gordon died in 1982, and is buried at the ancient Kincardine church in Strathspey.

David Gordon is Huntly Gordon's youngest son, by his second marriage. Born in 1956, he was educated at Sherborne and Sandhurst. He has been a soldier, an environmental lobbyist and a county councillor. A lifelong campaigner on environmental issues, his passions also include restoring and conserving old vehicles and old houses. He lives in rural Somerset.

B/112

13